YOU'RE ON THE THE VERGE OF SOMETHING BIG

y

SAY YES QUICKLY BOOKS

7715 East Highland Avenue

Scottsdale, Arizona, 85251, USA

Cover photograph by Dominik Hofbauer / Unsplash.

Author photograph by Phil Crozier.

ISBN: 979-8-9898660-5-2

First paperback edition.

ROSHNI DAYA

YOU'RE ON THE THE VERGE OF SOMETHING BIG

FINDING THE JOY
AND AUTHENTICITY
ALREADY INSIDE YOU

y

SAY YES QUICKLY BOOKS

Contents

for Keiran and Mira

To see a World in a Grain of Sand
And a Heaven in a Wild Flower
Hold Infinity in the palm of your hand
And Eternity in an hour

— William Blake

Prologue

A few weeks ago, a beautiful man walked into my life. This sounds like the beginning of a love story, and in a way it is. Not your ordinary, romantic love story, but a tale of the power of love to create the change we are seeking. It is also a story of deep pain and inner confusion. This is our story—yours and mine—a story each of us lives every day.

Seeking advice, I offered this man—an expert in coaching, marketing, and the self-help industry—a manuscript of the book you are about to read. He gave me some great feedback, the most important of which was telling me that *I had not done enough to disturb the pain*. And he was right. This thing called the "human condition"—a fancy way of saying "pain"—is what binds us. We relate through the pain we don't want to admit is there. When we share our struggles, we are looking for comfort and connection. We want to know we're not alone in this big world and at the same time, be assured that we are unique. And not just unique, but here on this planet for a purpose. We want to step into something larger than what we have known because we desire a real way out of this pain, a way that is not just another distraction.

As I write these words, I feel the tears stream down my face for the sense of desperation I have felt so often in my life. Few things have worked out the way I once had hoped, including a painful relationship with my parents, a failed marriage, and parenting alone. And these are only a few of my "failures". I believed my life would be easier. I believed I knew better than others, and that I only needed to do things the right way to achieve happiness. I kept believing I would be happy if I could just make something happen that I wanted desperately to happen. Yet, each time I arrived at that destination, I felt only a fleeting moment of happiness followed by another letdown. I had fallen into the same trap as many others—looking outside myself for something to distract me from my pain. (I have a large and beautiful boot collection to show for the years I spent in that process!)

My message isn't sexy. I'm not selling wealth, beauty, fame, or romance. I'm offering a new way of experiencing life that requires you to face the place where you are and what you have as a starting point. This process requires you to see that life is a process and that there are no outcomes. It is a journey to the place where you understand that you are at the centre of your lived experience, and although your lived experience may feel very narrow and painful now, there is a richer, fuller lived experience that lies within you awaiting discovery. Only by growing into the place where you are, are you able to experience what you have with peace and acceptance.

There is something more, "something big" as I call it. That something big is not an *outcome*. It is not arriving somewhere and standing tall because you made it.

Something big is falling in love with your child, and I mean deeply in love every time you look at her, no matter how old she is. Something big is having the first sip of your morning coffee and tasting it with every part of yourself, becoming one with the joy of that pleasure.

Something big is feeling the depth of pain when you lose a loved one without fear or avoidance. Something big is meeting every single moment of every day with your whole self because the only thing real in that moment is *that moment*. If fame or wealth or great romance is in your cards, my joy for you is that you will experience it in its entirety. It's not about the fame, or wealth, or romance, but about the capacity to experience whatever we have so we can meet what will come next.

Let me tell you a little about myself. I'm of East Indian descent, the second generation to live in Canada. I was born in Cape Town, South Africa and immigrated to Toronto with my parents and younger brother at the age of three. With little money or education and two young mouths to feed, my parents decided a business was their best means of survival. Our family's convenience store in our new city's central core was open from 9 a.m. to 11 p.m., seven days a week. I grew up behind a cash register in the years before registers told you how much change to return to the customer. My math skills were, and remain, well honed!

My parents had moved to a new country halfway around the world from the country where they grew up under a system of apartheid. How could they not be frightened? In fact, my very strict parents lived life from a place of fear, one learned from their parents. Fearful people control, and as a result I grew up in a controlled and controlling environment.

And yet, what courage it must have taken to get on a plane and move to a foreign country in search of a better life! I'm not sure I could do the same. So much courage and so much fear, at the same time. How often do we let ourselves feel two contradictory emotional experiences at once? Almost never. Strangely, we confine ourselves to one feeling at a time, while also acting as though the allowed range of feelings is very narrow. As a result, we expend a lot of energy trying *not* to feel, which steals from us the great potential richness of human experience.

Looking back, I can't say I had a "normal" Canadian childhood. I went to school and worked with my parents in their various businesses. I spent little or no time with friends or going to the playground or doing the other things kids do. I read a lot. Believing a good education was my road to the freedom they lacked, my parents pushed me to spend every spare moment doing something "productive." Under the influence of my parents' East Indian heritage and cultural background, I lived within the strictures of many rules about right and wrong, along with relentless pressure to avoid bringing shame to the family. Looking back now, I see that adolescent behaviours considered pretty normal in the society around me carried shame within my family and culture. As a teen, receiving a phone call from a boy, for instance, would result in huge conflict within our home. The fact that a boy had called me could only mean I was a "bad" girl doing "bad" things.

Desperate nevertheless for my parents' approval, I was beyond compliant. The fire within me today was as yet barely a flicker. As I came into my early twenties, our home environment became increasingly tumultuous.

Then, at twenty-three, following a series of traumatic events, I embarked on a backpacking trip with friends to India, where, despite my heritage, I had never been.

Adjanta and Elora are small, ancient towns in central India, famous for their caves housing paintings of ancient scriptures, illustrations, and Hindu and Buddhist carvings. Arriving in the monsoon season with few other tourists about, somehow I found myself alone in a large cave containing a huge statue of the Buddha—and nothing more. The moment I entered this cave, time stood still. I sat down and wept. I wept for all my years of despair, trying to be the daughter my parents so desperately wanted and needed me to be. I wept for the pressure of trying to be someone I wasn't. I wept for the pain of not being seen—and not seeing myself. I was a young adult, but I was so filled with doubt. A lifetime of trying to please had left me empty and alone. I wept for the little girl I once was and the quashing of my beautiful spirit. Years of repressed pain that had made me judgmental, righteous, and arrogant came pouring out, and I was held in a spirit I knew was my home.

Soon after, travelling in another part of India, I became so sick I nearly died and had to be hospitalized for a few days. That experience, following so shortly after that day in the cave, left me with the conclusion I, in fact, did die. The old me, committed to untruth, fear, and pleasing others at all costs, was gone.

Instead of referring to it as an awakening, I think of it as a remembering. To me, an awakening means moving out of the dark into the light. We awaken each day. We emerge from the night to meet the dawn. The truth is, however, we don't meet each day new. We carry the repressed pain of days and weeks into the new day, so we rarely awaken to a new day full of fresh and new possibilities.

Our new days are carryovers from the day before and the day before that. Only when we have dealt with that which we have repressed through an awakening process can we *truly* awaken to a new day of possibilities.

To *remember*, by contrast, is to come back to something we once knew. In order to awaken, we have to first *remember*. A long time, even a decade, may pass between our remembering and our awakening, but it is still necessary for a remembering to occur first. That is what occurred in the cave.

What is it that we have to remember? We have to remember we are not just the story we are living. We are not the culmination of the pain we have trapped and the patterns we have developed to avoid that pain. We have to remember that we were born full of the promise of a complete experience of life. We are not all meant to be famous, or brilliant, or models. That stuff doesn't matter. What we *are* all meant to experience is life in its range of depth, beauty, brilliance, pain, sorrow, joy, ecstasy, and, sometimes, its agony.

That is what I remembered that day in the cave. I remembered I was living the wrong way. On the way from that place to where I am today, I took many painful and tumultuous roads. That was my process. I learned. And now I am a Spiritual Teacher.

What does it mean to "come home?" Did I come home to the homeland of my heritage? Did I come home to myself? Did I come home to contact with a power greater than myself? I don't know. Maybe one, maybe all of those. All I know is that when we remember, we come home. Maybe a divinity resides deep inside each of us. Maybe coming home means making deep contact with oneself after long being elsewhere. Does it matter what we call it? You will recognize "coming home," which is a friend of remembering, when you feel it.

When I returned to my parents in Toronto, I began to move through a series of changes. First, I allowed myself to know I did not want to work as a lawyer despite having just completed a law degree and year of apprenticeship. Next, I worked on applications to graduate school in the field of psychology, a long-time passion of mine. As a bonus, post-graduate study would allow me to step away from the intense pressure I was receiving to get married. These were difficult days for me, and I'm a little embarrassed to admit that it took another twenty years for me to face the pain of the disapproval and rejection I received every time I took a stand for what I wanted or believed in. I understood that my parents loved me and wanted what they believed was best for me, but I wanted something different, even if I wasn't yet clear about what that was. I was often scared and so hurt I wasn't sure I could get up and face the day ahead. But I also felt courage, strength, and a degree of excitement I had never felt before.

All this triggered fear and shame in my parents and led to much destruction in our family. And here's another painful truth about the awakening that follows remembering. Awakening is the *commitment* to that which we remember. First, we remember that we are more than a vehicle for others to get what they want. We remember that there is a rich experience of life waiting for us in each and every moment. But *how* do we get from where we are to the way we would like to travel?

The "how" is the process of awakening. It requires us to be aware of ourselves and to do what needs to be done in order to break free of destructive patterns we have adopted. And here is where external messages about selfishness begin. I received a lot of messages about my selfishness, and those were very hard years. But it is not selfish to think of oneself. It is selfish to use others to fill ourselves up. It is selfish to blame others for our shortcomings. It is selfish to control others even if we have good intentions. It is selfish to hold others back because of our need for comfort and familiarity. To know yourself and what you want from life is not selfish even if it is at odds with what others want for you. The messages we receive about being selfish are frequently a reflection of the beliefs of the messenger. In my case, I was in pursuit of myself and very determined. The fire ignited in the cave kept burning inside me, and through much of this period I felt like a warrior.

I completed my master's degree and moved on to my doctorate. By now, time was ticking, and I wanted to get married—to a person of my choice. I chose a man who was the opposite of the extreme control I experienced with my parents, someone with little control over his life. As a child, I had experienced great pressure to succeed, so I chose someone who was not at all driven. My ex-husband and I were not well matched and spent many years hurting each other. We were two people playing out our shadow tendencies, having each chosen someone who represented the opposite of what they had known growing up.

Tense relationship with parents, failed marriage. And it was a marriage I had chosen. I had made my choice thinking I knew better. It was hard to swallow a failure like that. It was hard to work through facing my pride and to admit not just to myself but to the whole world that I really didn't know what I was doing. My grand plan for a better, more meaningful life had flopped. It was good for me to face all of that, however, because the process brought about the next big shift.

I had spent years pursuing an outcome, years pursuing my wholeness by trying to create ideal life circumstances, just as my parents had spent years pursuing their own wholeness through me. They really believed that if I were the daughter they wanted me to be, they would feel good, successful, proud, and accomplished.

I had done the same. I had believed that my wholeness lay outside of me, and that when everything lined up I would feel good, successful, proud, and accomplished. We all make the same mistakes, or, more accurately, we all engage in the same process. Some awaken within it, some don't. I accepted not just that I hadn't known better, but that I couldn't have known better. How could I know what I didn't know? I accepted that, although it wasn't my fault, it was my responsibility to do something different now that I was awakening.

This realization, however, did not take the bad feelings away, as I had hoped. Feelings we label "bad" are part of the human experience. We need to be able to feel them, in order to be informed about certain aspects of life. The objective is never to make the bad feelings go away, but instead to change our relationship with them. When we enhance our capacity to really feel those feelings, *they* let go of *us*.

Knowing I had made mistakes wasn't enough to create the shift that was needed for me to experience myself and my situation in a new way. I also had to be willing to accept that my beliefs were wrong. I had to admit I simply did not know what I was doing. I had to admit that quite possibly everything I believed about living was wrong. I had to clean my slate, and that was scary.

Without my beliefs about myself and my life—and all the judgments about who and where I should be—who was I? The end of my marriage was accompanied by such big questions.

I had finally arrived at the place I had sought from the beginning. This was the reason I had studied psychology. What I was really interested in was not so much *why* do we do what we do. I thought I had figured that one out for the most part. Now, I wanted to know *how*. *How* do we move ourselves from the paradigm that shackles us into the paradigm that liberates us? *How* do we let go of what we know in order to open ourselves to knowing something else? *How* do we evolve from being goal-oriented, outcome-driven people, to present-centred beings with the capacity to experience the fullness of life? These were the big, real questions. Not what or why, but how.

It is easy to look at something and analyze. We do it all the time and are pretty good at it. We're less good at figuring out how to make that something be something else. The reason? We focus on the thing itself. For example, if I see my child having repeated temper tantrums, I put a lot of effort into figuring out how to get him to stop. I'm less good at seeing those tantrums as an opening, or as a way of getting my attention. Life may have handed you a whole series of temper tantrums whose messages you have missed. Alternatively, an onslaught of temper tantrums may be underway right now. Once your attention is in the right place, the tantrums, no longer necessary, will stop.

In my self-discovery practice, with clients I went through a phase when I asked my adult clients if they had *felt* loved by their parents as they grew up, if they *knew* their parents loved them, or both. I was trying to get at whether most people's experience of that love was a *cognitive* idea or a *feeling* experience.

Nearly to a person they replied that they knew their parents loved them but had not felt the love. I realized that most of us pass the same experience onto our own children. The same can be said for the relationship between life partners. After the initial falling-in-love stage, most people will say they know their partner loves them, but that they don't feel loved. The story is much the same when people consider their love for themselves. Self-judgment and self-criticism do not come from a place of love.

If fear is standing in the way of love, and judgment is standing in the way of facing the fear, we must acknowledge the truth first. Whatever we are feeling in any given moment is the truth today. And we are in motion, so the truth of the experience in this moment will give way to the truth of experience in another moment. We can't access love without facing and working through whatever is standing between the current experience of life and the experience of love. This is where I want to take you. Not to where you feel only love and nothing else; that would get boring. But to a place where you feel all of it and can therefore feel love, too.

When you enter into that empowering space, able to comfortably and bravely feel all of it, you can choose which emotion to embrace.

Falling in love is the easiest thing in the world to do. When we enter into an experience with another person and that experience holds novelty, openness, and curiosity, we give ourselves permission to enter fully into the present moment. Time seems to stand still. There is nothing in that moment but you and the person with whom you are sharing that space. Love breaks through all the other feelings only when you can enter into that encounter that way. We get present with another being and love emerges between us. If we got present with ourselves, drinking coffee or tea, listening to the birds, looking at the eyelashes of our child, love would also emerge—not because we are in love with coffee or birds or eyelashes but because our focused presence allows love to be revealed.

Presence enables you to contact your capacity to love, but the capacity to love need not involve another being in order to be accessed and experienced. It begins with you, loving you. You know that. What life is giving you is not nearly as important as how you meet it. I want you to have a choice in how you meet what life is bringing, and this book is designed to lead you through a process that gives you that choice.

The end of my marriage created an opening for me to blow everything up inside so that I could die and be born new with openness, curiosity, and an attitude of novelty towards life. By allowing yourself to see this pain—the pain you are experiencing right now—you will see that the hardest thing you face is simultaneously the best thing life is offering right now. Rest assured you should not and could not have known better sooner. We do what we know until we realize we don't actually know anything. It sucks, but that is how it works.

In this book you will read much about the *why*, but also the *how* of the journey process. My motivation for writing has never been wealth or fame but simply a strong belief there is something big here that can help. My motivation comes from knowing that most people in the world, no matter what walk of life, struggle with the same pain. I have personally journeyed through every process outlined in this book. And I know I can only go deeper, learn more, through sharing what I know. That is part of my journey.

For a movement to get going, a single guide must shine the light. My hope as a guide is that others will engage in their own processes and revelations, and together we can build upon the foundation laid down here. Students become teachers who inform more students who become teachers, and so on.

As the first guide, however, I must also be able to receive whatever comes with the role. I have no idea what that will be and admit the thought of it makes me very uncomfortable. Many of us spend much of our lives feeling some degree of fear, reflected mainly in worries about the future. We are afraid of what we don't want. But I have also realized we are equally afraid of what we do want. To accept what we want requires us to receive, and to receive is one of life's most vulnerable experiences.

Some time ago, a friend helped me understand I had trouble allowing the work I was doing at that time to enter the world and create the energy and movement of which it was capable. The obstacle was that I did not know how to receive the attention or recognition that would come with the process. In considering this, I realized I had spent a lifetime trying to prepare for not getting what I wanted and *never* thinking about getting what I did want.

Receiving is difficult for me, and I'm not good at it. This is my growing edge. Still, I want these pages to guide you. Even though I am afraid, I am still going to put one foot in front of the other and move myself through the version of that fear my parents held when they embarked on a new life in an unfamiliar place.

If you are afraid, be afraid. Give yourself permission to know what is really happening inside you rather than judging yourself for your fear. Once you get honest, you have no need for judgment. It no longer serves its escapist purpose and lets go of you. There's nothing wrong with any emotion in the world, only *not allowing* the emotion. Remember, too, that feelings and actions are two separate things. Having a feeling neither necessitates nor justifies any particular action arising from the feeling. So get real with yourself.

I have shared with you some parts of myself and set the stage for the book's content. The most important piece of advice I can give at this stage is that you will not understand what is happening until it has happened. You are about to embark on a journey outside of your current paradigm. When you try to *understand*, you get in your own way and fail to evolve. If you are willing to *experience* and *engage* in the process, you will evolve and understand later, perhaps better than I. If that happens, please contact me and share. I would love to learn from you.

You're On the Verge of Something Big

INTRODUCTION

D o you ever feel—or wish you could feel—you're on the verge of something big? Do you have the intuition that an inner shift is about to take place, a shift that could lead to profound change in your life? You want change, need change, yet you can't make that change happen. You know you're stuck inside patterns that keep you feeling life is hard.

What if any given moment in life could lead you to that somewhere big? What if you could find the place inside that feels like you and let go of worrying what others think of you? What if you could let go of wondering what might happen in the future and leave behind the stories of the past? What if you could quiet your mind, release yourself from all the messages about how you should be?

What if you could understand what stands between you and your true self? What if you could see clearly where that endless internal dialogue comes from, that dialogue that keeps you feeling insecure, unsure, and generally fearful? What if you could find practices that would allow you to move past all the stuck places within and emerge with the capacity to know yourself, the true you? What if you could surrender the future, the past, old regrets and anticipatory worries, and become present enough in each life moment to experience true joy?

As a spiritual teacher, I have travelled the terrain of the thousands of times with thousands of clients. Each life story is unique. Yet the patterns hidden within the stories are universal. As unique as each of us wants to be, our uniqueness does not lie in the story patterns of our lives. It lies within our authentic self, the self that was intended to show up for the life we are in. We have become so attached to our life stories that we are stuck within them. That "stuckness" is what prevents us from meeting our true selves. It prevents us from getting out of the stories in our minds so that we can meet the moment fully. It steals our joy—not happiness, which is fleeting and often tied to outside circumstance—but joy, a feeling deep within, that is a friend of peace, acceptance and love.

The gift that the thousands of clients I've worked with have given me is the revelation of the patterns of "stuckness." Once a pattern is identified, something can be done about it. It moves from the unconscious, the place where we don't know what we are doing, to the conscious, the place where we become aware of more of our selves—our thoughts, our emotions, and our physical experience. When we are aware of more of our experience in any given moment, we begin for the first time in our lives to have choice. It might sound a little dramatic to read that we have choice for the first time in our lives. But if you take a moment and reflect on how difficult it is to break a habit, you might concede that we *think* we are choosing more than we actually do. Most of the time, the unconscious patterns in which we are stuck, choose for us. Making those unconscious patterns conscious through the journey outlined here is part of the excitement. Liberation from the patterns will allow you to experience life in a way you never imagined possible. Via that liberation, the unique you, waiting to meet life will burst out of you in joy.

When you are free from the patterns, all of life is different—every relationship, every interaction, every moment. This doesn't mean everything goes your way all the time. Far from it. Plenty will go your way, and lots will not. *Happiness* may be tied to life going your way. *Joy* is showing up for life in your authentic self and meeting the tough moments with the same openness and acceptance as the easy ones.

Back to patterns. When you assist people through their life struggles, you come to learn a lot about their inner workings. I have learned that most of us worry about the same sorts of things. We worry about what others think of us. We play over conversations in our minds and try to decipher minuscule signals from others to figure out what they are thinking about us. We worry about whether we are liked and accepted and have trouble when we conclude we are not. We worry about what the future holds for us. Just as we replay tiny events of the past, we play forward what might happen the future. We worry about all the possible outcomes of our efforts in order to be prepared for those events. We do this sort of thing in most of our relationships. We do it in relation to close family members as well as acquaintances. Somehow, it seems we don't know how to stop engaging in these patterns of thinking.

On top of this worry focused on others, the past, and the future—and even more to our detriment—we spend much mental energy doing one of two problematic things. First, we tell ourselves we should not be feeling the way we do, whether we are angry or sad or afraid. "I have no right to be sad. There are people in the world whose problems are much worse than mine." "I shouldn't be angry. I should be kind and considerate." "I have no reason to feel afraid." We dismiss every emotional experience, believing we have no right to our feelings. This puts us at war with ourselves.

Second, we justify or rationalize how we feel: "Here are all the reasons I have a right to feel angry, hurt." We don't actually feel the experience. Instead, our minds get very busy telling ourselves over and over again that we have a right to the feelings. "I'm very fearful about the future since my wife lost her job. How can I not be afraid that we might have to move to a different city? This is a terrible thing and I have no control over it." "I am so angry at my husband. He takes me for granted. I do everything around here and he doesn't even seem notice."

The most significant pattern I have observed within myself and all my clients is the pattern of moving between dismissing the emotional experience and rationalizing it. All that worry about the thoughts and feelings of others, the past, and the future falls within a pattern of dismissing or rationalizing the emotional experience.

I first observed these patterns most clearly within myself. With the practice of mindfulness meditation, I began to notice that my mind kept me very busy, either telling me how I should be or informing me of the many reasons I had a right to feel the way I did. More importantly, I started to notice I was stuck inside these patterns of thinking. The same patterns kept emerging even as the subject of my stories changed, based upon the events of my life at the time. Sometimes the stories were about my family, other times about office colleagues or friends.

I also noticed that even when I felt justified in my feelings, I felt stuck inside them—as though I wasn't processing them. I wasn't able to, as they say, "let them go." I knew I was supposed to let things go, but I couldn't. The emotions were as stuck as I was in the thoughts about them. Through observing myself closely in my meditative practice, I could see that thought patterns—dismissing or rationalizing the emotions—were interfering with the process of "letting go" of the emotional experience. I started to observe this same process in every client I worked with. We all seemed to be going round and round inside our thoughts, somehow trapping our emotional experience in the process.

Determined to understand how these universal patterns came to be, I experienced a huge *aha!* moment. In a flash, I was able to see how the problematic process was created, patterned, and was interfering with not only the experience of daily life for everyone I encountered, but also how we humans are stuck in an evolutionary capacity to come together as one species. By examining its individual components, I was able to piece together the bigger picture. I came to understand how this extremely significant problem in our evolutionary development is hindering us from being our true selves. I came to see how, when we as individuals don't permit ourselves to be our true selves, the outcome is a world in which we are pitted against each other. The battle within ourselves is perfectly reflected in our battle with each other.

Through ongoing work within myself and with my clients, the road out of this patterning also became clear. It has been tested over and over again, and it works! There is a way to align oneself with oneself, and in doing so, to align every human with humanity as a whole.

When something is authentic, it is the real thing. It's not disguised, altered, or changed into something else. When a person is authentic, she is in her truth. She is able to be who she really is without worrying about what others think or feel about her. We are driven to be other than our authentic self by complex mechanisms that I will describe in later chapters. But at the root of it all, we are looking for love and acceptance. When we don't allow ourselves to be ourselves, it is because deep down inside we believe that we have to be what the other person wants us to be in order to be loved and accepted by that other person. We all do it, and we all learn how to do it in childhood.

Our greatest needs in life are love and acceptance, and they are at the centre of the healing process that takes us out of the inner battle and transforms us into integrated, whole beings. The authentic person has changed her relationship with herself from self-harming to self-love and self-acceptance. Self-harming is an act of negativity towards oneself. Negative things you say to yourself are acts of self-harm. Telling yourself you should be a certain way is an act of self-harm. So many of us spend all day harming ourselves in our inner world. And when we do this all day, every day, we lose track of who we are. Each of us is so lost in our unique style of self-harming inner dialogue we have no idea who we would be if we stopped and accepted ourselves just as we are in this moment.

The you that you are when you accept yourself in this moment is your authentic self.

My client, the youngest of four siblings, was working on this process with me. Simon talked about his chameleon nature, how he had a self in the city where he attended university and a different self when he visited his parents in the city where he grew up. His speech was full of phrases like, "I know I should . . . " and "I know I shouldn't . . . ". Whenever he talked about his relationship with his family members, he was full of painful feelings such as anger, hurt, irritation, annoyance, sadness, fear, and worry. Every time Simon mentioned how he felt, he concluded the statement with, "I know I shouldn't feel this way" or "I really do love my mom/dad/brother." He told me that when friends discussed their own problems with him, he would give advice about compassion and forgiveness, but that no matter how hard he tried to feel these emotions for his own family he could not. Simon would then engage in a pattern of inner negativity about his failure to be more kind towards his family. He lamented that it was too difficult to feel compassion and forgiveness and said he didn't actually believe anyone could feel this way. He believed that everyone goes around talking in this nice way while secretly harbouring negative feelings they can't get past. Most painful for Simon was that he felt that he did not have even one person in his life with whom he could be himself because *he* didn't know who he was.

This is a common plight. You may recognize aspects of yourself in Simon's struggle. How does one even begin to know his or her authentic self with all this inner turmoil going on?

Another client, a young woman who was also in university, spoke about feelings she had around her father's negative opinion of her chosen career path and her longing for his acceptance. She discussed all the ways she looked for his approval by hiding parts of herself she believed unacceptable.

The client's mother, Cindy, discussed her own feelings about marriage and raising children. She talked about her own childhood hopes and dreams, which she had never shared because of her belief that her cultural background would not allow for who she was inside. She talked about the feeling of betrayal by her parents, whom she felt had neither seen nor supported her in a fulfilling path. She felt trapped into being what she believed others wanted her to be. In her mid-fifties now, she continues to feel trapped—shackled to what she perceived others expected of her.

Perhaps these few examples contain elements similar to your own experience. You may relate quite strongly to the emotional pain felt by each of these three people: blame, anger, resentment, irritability, guilt, shame, worry, fear, sadness, grief, loss, unlovability, unworthiness, unacceptability. So much pain—all standing in the way of finding one's own truth—the truth of who one is beneath the pain, the truth blocked by the fear of being unlovable, unworthy, and unacceptable.

There is a "you" underneath all the pain, the same "you" that is in me. That "you" is in each one of us, universal and at the same time utterly unique. It is the "you" who knows that in order for any other love and acceptance to be felt, there must first come an honest facing of oneself, followed by acknowledgement and acceptance of what is. The journey inward outlined in this book will bring you to the authentic you. The authentic you is able to be clear about what you think and feel. The authentic you knows it is your responsibility to stand in that place of truth, no matter how difficult. The authentic you knows your opinion of you is more important than what you perceive other people to think about you. In fact, the authentic you knows that, since you actually have no control over what others think and feel about you, you need not concern yourself with it. The authentic you feels that place of inner wisdom and truth so deeply it becomes easier to honour than betray. The authentic you is in love with you. The most beautiful part of the journey to the authentic self is the deep acceptance one feels for herself. At the heart of that love and acceptance is a peace so profound and still that true joy can be felt for the first time.

This does not mean others will fall into step with the authentic you. There will be some who will celebrate you in your truth, as they have been waiting to meet the authentic you for a long time. Others will put pressure on you to be who they want you to be. Don't worry, their lives will change as a result of you standing in your truth. That is their responsibility, not yours.

As you journey to your true self, you will go through a process of self-alignment. Like the three clients I described above, you have spent years in a battle with yourself. As you begin to align with yourself—that is, work through the inner battle—things outside of you will also change to reflect that. At first, the battles you avoided on the outside by betraying yourself will come into some focus. You'll become aware of the inner toll it has taken to continually present yourself to others in the way you believed they wanted. As you work through the inner battling process and move toward inner alignment, there may be some tension in your everyday life as it adjusts to the changes you are making.

As Simon moved through his inner conflicts, he found that all his feelings were transformed. As he acknowledged each one and accepted the truth of his experience in the moment, Simon was able to meet himself. He also learned to meet himself with love and acceptance of what was in his inner world—no matter how negative and painful. Everything shifted and, over time, he moved into a natural state of compassion and forgiveness for the members of his family. And it surprised him. Simon's big question to me was, "How could this happen just by accepting the pain instead of fighting it?"

Authenticity is the truth. It is being with what is, as it is. No defenses, no desire for anything else, no judgment, no right or wrong, no good or bad. Just what is. When you are able to be this way with yourself, something big happens. Your heart opens up, first to yourself, then to others. Authenticity is all about care. It is not about standing up for yourself in a way that harms others. It is standing within yourself, in the centre of yourself, with so much love and acceptance of yourself that your heart overflows with love and acceptance for others, too.

This is true even if the other cannot meet you there. It's not about what the other does or does not do to you. This journey to authenticity requires you to be so entirely responsible for yourself that you will never be able to blame another human being, life event, or circumstance again. You will see that within every experience is an opportunity to deepen your capacity to love the parts of yourself that are so dark you don't even want to admit they exist. This is the excitement of the journey. You will come to know yourself in a way you never imagined. In the process, your heart will expand and you will learn to love in a way you didn't know was even possible. That is the authentic truth.

In the pages ahead I hope to guide you to a deeper understanding of the same problematic inner process discovered by my clients. You will come to understand how and why it developed. You will see how you got stuck in certain patterns and understand why the part of you working against you believes it is protecting you. You will be guided through a process that will help wake you up to yourself and recognize the patterns running your life. You will learn how to awaken the authentic self within to take its rightful place as the leader of *you*. Finally, you will be shown how, through personal transformation, you become involved in global transformation.

So, you decide. Are you on the verge of something big?

Part One: Figuring Yourself Out

The Sabre-Toothed Tiger

1

Humans, like other animals, have what is known as a "fight-flight" response to events in the world around them. In our brains, certain hormones control how we respond to perceived danger: should we get ready to duke it out or run away and hide in a cave until the danger passes?

Imagine a lizard basking quietly on a warm rock. Suddenly, it senses a change in temperature, a shadow between itself and the sun. The lizard opens his eyes, only to see a bigger reptile looking at him hungrily. The lizard's fight-flight system is activated immediately and dramatically. Based on years of history, the lizard is very quickly able to determine that, in this instance, it better get out of there. He flees to a nearby rock and squeezes into a space large enough for him, but not his predator, to fit. Once the danger passes, the lizard's fight-flight response calms and he gets back to the business of eating bugs under the rock.

We are like lizards, only more complex. In hunting-and-gathering times, we might have looked up while we were sorting through the nourishing plants we had gathered and seen a sabre-toothed tiger looking hungrily at us. Our fight-flight response would have been activated, and we would have run, like the lizard, to a protective place. Once the danger passed, our fight-flight system would calm and we would return to everyday survival.

We have developed in both capacity and complexity since primitive times, but some glitches in the system occurred. And they interfere deeply with our ability to *be* in the present moment, show up in life authentically, and to fully experience joy. Here's where the problems lie.

In addition to having a fight-flight system, we also have emotions, or what I call the "emotional body." We also carry memory, perception, and the capacity to reason. This complexity gives us the ability to do amazing things in life. But it also sometimes causes us to get a bit mixed up. Instead of becoming integrated, the systems become conflicted. This is what has happened to most people—all because of our deep need for love and acceptance and our fear that we will never feel loved and accepted.

Part of you might choose to argue with these words. You might be thinking, "But I do feel loved and accepted," or "I know that my parents love me." You might be wondering, "How can a whole system get messed up because of love and acceptance? I don't really need those feelings to function." These defensive thoughts and feelings perfectly illustrate the point. If you are not feeling defensive, you've already managed to get through a part of the process. You will not have recoiled at the words written here. But the malfunction exists for every single human being. It is a universal experience. If it does not exist for you at this time in your life, it's because you have already reprogrammed the patterning in your brain that went astray very early in life.

Our brilliance as humans lies in those parts of ourselves I have mentioned: our emotional body, our perception, our memory, and our capacity to reason or think. Here's where things have taken a wrong turn for us. Because we have an emotional body, perception, and memory, our fight-flight centre is often activated for reasons other than physical danger. We have an inner world experience of *perceived* emotional danger. For most humans, in fact, our greatest threat in the context of daily life is perceived emotional danger.

Emotional dangers are many, and the biggest of them is the feeling of being unloved, unaccepted, and unworthy. This means every time I feel someone might not like me or might not like what I say about my thoughts or feelings, I risk feeling unloved, unaccepted, or unworthy. Every time I interact with another human being, I run the risk of being unloved, unacceptable, or unworthy. Worse, I also run the risk of *perceiving* myself to be unloved and unaccepted. After all, everything gets filtered through my own lens or perception. My fight-flight system can be activated and I can believe I'm in emotional danger simply by the way a person looks at me, by his tone of voice or his lack of attentiveness, or *simply by my own perception of the situation*.

Next, I have a memory. The fight-flight centre doesn't actually know whether an event is happening in real time or in my memory. It responds in the same way—with a slight change in intensity. So, I go through my day, living through a series of moments of feeling real or perceived emotional danger—feeling unloved, unaccepted, or unworthy. On my own again, my brain won't shut off. It plays events over and over in my mind and projects into the future based on these now-past events.

So, even now, away from the interaction my fight-flight centre remains activated. I still feel that I'm in emotional danger.

This paints a slightly more complete picture, but there is actually even more happening here. Our capacity to reason causes us to engage in one of two ways. Either we get busy dismissing and denying our emotional experience (which does nothing to stop that experience) or we get busy rationalizing our experiences of emotional danger (which may lead to granting ourselves permission to engage in harmful actions toward those we perceive to be responsible for that danger).

How we act depends on how we choose to deploy our reasoning skills. If we are dismissive of our experience, we tend to engage in life in a fairly passive way. If we are caught up in rationalizing and justification, we tend to be more aggressive toward others. Either way, our fight-flight system remains activated. Either way, by denial or rationalization, our feelings of being unloved, unacceptable, and unworthy actually become deepened.

Now, back to the sabre-toothed tiger—who cavemen probably didn't encounter very often. Their fight-flight response to the tiger was activated in acute situations for relatively short, contained periods of time—survive or die. Physical survival in that case required skill and speed. Our problem today is that the sabre-tooth has moved from the real to the perceived. He has become the whole brain with its emotional body, perception, memory and reasoning. In short, the sabre-toothed tiger lives inside us.

Every time we feel in emotional danger, we encounter the sabre-tooth tiger. Every time we remember a time of emotional danger, we encounter the sabre-tooth. Every time we reason ourselves through the experience, we encounter the sabre-tooth. The sabre-toothed tiger is in our minds, and it is making us crazy. By identifying with all our thought processes, we have come to think we *are* the sabre-tooth tiger. Instead of understanding that we possess a *true self* that is separate from the sabre-tooth tiger, we have come to believe we are *only* the sabre-tooth. That is why authenticity confuses us.

My Journey with the Sabre-Tooth

When I began my inward journey figuring this out, all I knew was that I was miserable. I thought I had many good reasons to be miserable because of the hard things I had been through. I was negative, angry, resentful, hurt, and I vacillated between justifying and dismissing my feelings. The truth was that I was stuck inside the sabre-toothed tiger in my mind.

As sophisticated as my inner language was (and I happen to have a well-educated, eloquent sabre-toothed tiger), I wasn't actually processing the pain and certainly not letting go of it. I identified myself as an intellectual meditator who could speak beautifully about compassion, letting go, being present, and opening one's heart. My sabre-toothed tiger had studied well, precisely knowing the identity most appealing to me, giving me lots of ways to talk about my life story. The more I listened to the stories of the sabre-tooth, the more stuck I became inside the pain, cut off from myself. My sabre-toothed tiger could take on the persona of a kind and caring pussycat, but in my personal life it was full-on tiger.

I decided no more reading, no more analyzing, no more trying to intellectualize what was going on in me. Only then did I begin to truly journey inward. I had no idea about authenticity. My whole life had been about trying to prove I was worthy of love and acceptance. As a result, I have four academic degrees. How many degrees did I *need* to figure this out? My journey inward showed me—probably none.

So, instead of getting lost in sabre-tooth's stories, stories that kept me in fight-flight mode, I began to watch myself. I wasn't skilled enough yet to do anything about what I was observing, but I could watch. No one else could see what I was doing, but I knew I was studying myself. I was studying universal human patterns embodied in me. I was studying how that sabre-toothed tiger spoke, what it said, how I listened, and what caused me to have a sabre-toothed tiger in the first place.

My biggest *aha!* came when I discovered that, while the sabre-tooth had me perceiving relationships as a threat to my emotional safety, it understood itself to be my friend. Sabre-tooth believed that I—the true "I"—couldn't cope with life all by myself. Sabre-tooth was trying to protect me from the pain of feeling , unacceptable, and unworthy.

I began to see that it wasn't actually important whether or not those feelings were true. The sabre-toothed tiger I had created and spent my whole life feeding believed I couldn't handle the pain of those emotional experiences. She had spent her whole life trying to protect me from them.

This journey was all about meeting my pain and nurturing myself. I had to find a way to encounter the unlovable, unacceptable, and unworthy within me and truly *love* them. I had to find a way to meet me as I am now and hold my heart open to that me in order to be truly *me*.

This is authenticity. When it began to blossom, the sabre-toothed tiger—previously wild and fierce and on constant guard—calmed down and chilled out. She began to rightfully inform me when I was in real physical or emotional danger so I, the real I, could do something about it.

Sabre-Tooth's Many Faces

Remember, your sabre-tooth is not your enemy. It wants a full and rich life for you but has only a tiger's capacity to create it. It's pretty limited and is happy with some flesh to chew on. It doesn't know about love, acceptance, nurturing, or joy. It doesn't know that when that fight-flight centre is calm, you can achieve your best physical, mental, emotional, and spiritual health. It doesn't know it is interfering with all that. Until now, you didn't know you even had a sabre-toothed tiger running your life, much less what to do about it. Nonetheless, despite believing it is a friend, sabre-tooth is a problem.

I have come into contact with thousands of sabre-toothed tigers. You, the real you, picked up this book by listening to a deeply intuitive and wise place in your heart, a place where you understand that there is more to life that the life you are experiencing now. As you read these words, the sabre-toothed tiger will read with you. It worries about you and fears for the pain you might feel. It is here to protect—and protect it will do. The voice in your head that makes you struggle against the path ahead of you is the voice of the sabre-toothed tiger.

Just as the wiser you picked up this book, the wiser self of my clients brings them to the self-discovery process. They come knowing there is something outside of this survival experience in which they are stuck. They bring their sabre-toothed tiger into the meetings and it is with us during our time together. This is how I have come to be an expert on sabre-toothed tigers. I began by getting to know my own; only later did I get to know thousands of others.

Sarah lost her father when she was a child. She grew up with younger siblings and a mother with whom she became an emotional partner. She worried about her mother's pain from the death of her father. She worried about not having enough money; she worried about her siblings and getting them to school. She basically raised her siblings and then, later, raised a family of her own. Her young life was a difficult one, in part because no one noticed the pain she was in. There was no time for that.

Because of her early life, Sarah's sabre-toothed tiger perceives all relationships as an emotional threat. It tells her no one cares about *her* thoughts and opinions. It tells her she isn't important to others. As a result, she treats herself as if her thoughts and opinions are not important. Her sabre-toothed tiger has trained others to treat her in exactly the way that confirms this story. Better for her to be angry than feel the real pain of a father who left her and a mother too busy simply surviving to notice her pain. Her sabre-toothed tiger believes it is better for her to be angry and resentful towards a husband who isn't interested in her than for her to feel unloved, unaccepted, and unworthy. And Sarah was stuck in this place.

Luke, a wealthy businessman and family man, was raised to meet the needs of others. He spent his whole life making sure his wife's and children's needs were all met. His sabre-toothed tiger made him believe that the way for him to be liked or loved was to make sure others were happy. So, he was always attentive to others. Every time he went into a business meeting, he did his best to gauge what others wanted so they would think he was a nice guy. He often apologized for himself.

Luke didn't begin his self-discovery journey until everything began to fall apart. His sabre-toothed tiger's "Mr. Nice Guy" strategy was no longer working. His marriage was ending and his children were blaming him. He didn't understand how all this could happen because he had spent his whole life trying to meet other people's needs rather than his own. Luke's sabre-toothed tiger made him believe that the bare illusion of love achieved by meeting other people's needs is better than the horror of being unloved, unaccepted, and unworthy if others discovered the real Luke. His sabre-toothed tiger kept him stuck inside that paradigm.

By her early thirties, Suzanne had had a series of relationships with men. She had also had a series of careers in her work life. Each of her intimate relationships was significant and meaningful and she engaged in each one fully until she believed the man was ready to commit to the relationship. Once he was committed, Suzanne would begin to stray. She would perceive a series of problems with her partner, then would engage in behaviours that led to the relationship's end.

Suzanne's sabre-toothed tiger was afraid—so terrified of being seen that when she began to get close to someone her tiger would tell her she didn't deserve to be loved, then persuade her that the man she was with was unworthy of a long term commitment. In the midst of all of this sabre-tooth chatter, Suzanne's behaviour within and outside the relationship would effectively doom the relationship. As she began to observe her sabre-toothed tiger, she also recognized the same pattern with career choices—the reason for her checkered work history as well. Suzanne's sabre-toothed tiger believed that the end of the relationship or work experience was less painful than feeling unlovable, unacceptable, and unworthy.

Chris was an extroverted, enthusiastic, and fairly charismatic man who could not sustain friendships or romantic relationships, although he tried. His natural charisma allowed him to engage with people and start relationships, but they all quickly ended. Chris' sabre-toothed tiger would not let him stop talking about himself.

He believed he had to be the centre of conversation, events, and situations at all times. His sabre-toothed tiger believed his survival was dependent on his always impressing everyone he met. In fact, his achievements were driven by his desire to talk about them later. Chris's sabre-toothed tiger believed he would achieve love and acceptance only by impressing others. His sabre-toothed tiger was deeply committed to giving him *pseudo* experiences of love, acceptance, and worthiness as a substitute for the potential pain of being alone.

Aaron was a middle-aged man who had not had much success in life. His marriage was thrust upon him, not a relationship he achieved for himself. He had not held a steady job for most of his adult life and was supported by his parents and wife. Aaron's sabre-toothed tiger kept him from properly looking for work and engaging in relationships. His sabre-toothed tiger believed his life circumstances were due to his painful childhood and that there was nothing he could do about that. He blamed his parents for not doing more. He blamed his siblings for getting all the attention and blamed his wife for making him feel bad about not being able to get a job. If anyone spoke with him about these issues, he either got very angry and verbally hurtful or he shut down the interaction entirely. Aaron's sabre-toothed tiger made him believe that not engaging in life was less painful than facing the pain of unlovability, unacceptability, and unworthiness.

As the above examples illustrate, each sabre-toothed tiger is unique, creative, and ingenious in its attempts to protect an individual from the pain of life. Each does a brilliant job. Each of our real selves does an equally excellent job of letting the sabre-tooth have its way. We hand ourselves over to its stories—and we even listen with great interest to the stories told by other people's sabre-tooths.

The stories are compelling, full of unique and interesting twists and turns, and yet after a while, we notice the stories repeat themselves. Their internal patterns are the same—all of them based on sadness and grief, fear and worry, shame and guilt, anger and resentment, blame, or overcoming one or all of the above by presuming some sort of superiority.

How Sabre-Tooth Creates Inner and Outer Conflict

Despite its attempts to be our friend, the sabre-toothed tiger serves to divide. First, it cuts us off from our own inner experience. Sabre-tooth's very existence rests on a belief that we cannot handle the world of experience that resides within us. It also divides us from others by having us believe others have the capacity to put us in emotional danger. It then allows us to rationalize our actions as necessary to protect ourselves from that threat. Perhaps you can identify myriad ways in which this process has played out in your life. You may recall the result: feeling alone and disconnected.

Now imagine a group of people who have come together because there is enough overlap in each of their sabre-tooth stories that their tigers feel a kind of kinship with one another. The nature of the tiger is to see enemies everywhere.

Soon other groups of people are a threat to the feelings and beliefs of this group. The threat must be extinguished. War ensues, tigers fighting tigers. This is what happens between nations, religious groups, and definitely also within families. Sabre-tooth feels threatened by the differences it perceives between itself and others. Groups feel that same threat, but in a more powerful and destructive way. When we allow our individual sabre-toothed tigers to run the show within ourselves, we unwittingly create and participate in the kind of world we have now—one full of enemies and in which we are more aware of the differences between our stories than the similarities within our hearts.

This inner division—the disconnect between mind and heart—is *often* reflected within families. The intolerance family members feel for one another is a reflection of the intolerance individuals within that family have for aspects of their own inner worlds. This path is not about changing others to be what we want them to be. Nor is it about changing ourselves to be what others think we should be. It is about coming to be with *what is*. Although we are all humans with the same heart, everything else about us is distinct. Therein lies our beauty. A world that is full of love and tolerance is a world in which sabre-tooth knows his place and we know ours.

If you continue to let it, your sabre-toothed tiger will run the show both inside you and out. By recognizing and acknowledging him, you can become aware of the patterns the tiger has developed to protect you from perceived emotional dangers. These patterns are based on the false belief that you can't handle the emotional experiences within.

Now that you know what's occurring inside, and how your own sabre-tooth came to take up residence, let's look more deeply at why.

Why Don't I Know Myself

2

It's astounding how little we know ourselves. Clients constantly tell me, "I don't know my truth," or "I don't know who I am," or "If I had to stop doing what I do, I would have no idea who I am." This struggle with knowing the self is the result of losing ourselves inside the stories of the sabre-toothed tiger. We keep busy thinking about all sorts of things that have much more to do with others' perceptions than with what we feel, think, and know for ourselves. We keep busy doing all sorts of things we really don't need to, driven by keeping up with what others are doing. Sabre-tooth has made it difficult to cut through the distraction created by our perception of success. We have been kept busy by that perception.

Why have we handed our whole experience of life over to the sabre-toothed tiger? Why have we allowed our fight-flight centre to remain so activated that we don't know how to experience our moment-to-moment existence without that false sense of survival taking over? Why have we allowed ourselves to endure the physical consequences of this overactive and out-of-control fight-flight mechanism?

The Immune System Response

When the fight-flight centre is activated, things occur within the physical body as well as the mind. We are a whole system, and the whole system responds to real or perceived threats. A message telling us we need to survive *right now* takes a huge toll on the body. It screams that there is a real-time threat and survival is essential. In all species, the body responds by taking energy away from secondary functions, such as digestion or reproduction, and pouring it into primary survival functions.

For human beings, a primary response in times of real or perceived threat takes place in the immune system, which is designed to fight bacterial and viral threats to the body. When we feel endangered, the body responds by charging up the immune system. The fastest rate of increase in disease in the modern world is in auto-immune disorders. "Auto-immune" is a broad umbrella term covering diseases in which the immune system attacks its own body. If the body receives the message that it is under attack, even if there is no real threat, the immune system releases that energy in its own counter-attack. That attack will take place in any area of genetic weakness. It may show up as allergies, thyroid or skin problems, cancer, reproductive struggles, or hundreds of other possibilities. This is how the mind and body are related—one system, all connected.

It is a problem that this goes on almost all the time. How did we ever get to this state and stay here for so long that all the body's systems are out of whack?

Nurturing: Being Versus Doing

I return to our need for love and acceptance. We are hard-wired for needing both. Every one of us is also born into a family environment. We are born to one or two parents who have lived their own set of life circumstances. Although each individual situation is unique, the need for love and acceptance through nurturing is not.

Nurturing is the experience of being seen, valued, and appreciated for who we truly are. Nurturing is not positive reinforcement for a job well done. Nurturing is not being told, "Good job!" for climbing the monkey bars or eating supper. Nurturing is respect and appreciation for the child's very being. And it is easy to get distracted from the being by the doing. That is part of why we get overly focused on goals. Goals are all about *doing*. That is why achieving or accomplishing goals does not fill that hole inside you. Accomplishing a goal means that you behaved well. Nurturing is valuing who you are, regardless of what you have achieved. Our need for nurturing is universal. It crosses cultures, generations, circumstances, and socio-economic differences. Every single being needs to be seen, valued, and respected simply for their being-ness.

"The reason you are the way that you are is because of your parents." Nope. You won't hear that from me. Your parents did the best they could. In most cases, that's a fact. Another fact is that *you had your own experience* within the context of your parents doing the best they could. And most of the time, if not always, your own experience left you feeling un-nurtured.

Your parents likely were raised with great emphasis on what they did or what they accomplished—and so they raised you the same way. You are probably passing that same emphasis on to your kids. Nobody is bad. But it's wise to remember that nurturing your child is not about cheering her on while she plays hockey and baseball and violin. Yes, being there in those settings is wonderful. But what your child really needs to feel is that even if she never played hockey, baseball or violin again, you would still see the bright light inside her and love her.

It's just the same as what your child self really wanted. You wanted your parent or parents to see you, not just what you were good at. You wanted your parent to let you know you were loved for who you were, regardless of whether you scored a goal.

While your well-intentioned parents did the best they could, you nonetheless still could have inner experiences of feeling un-nurtured . As a result, you could develop feelings of being unloved, unaccepted, and unworthy. I want to empha-size that both—a parent's good intentions *and* a child's feeling of being un-nurtured—can exist together, at the same time. In fact, they almost always do.

Our Personal Containers:
How They Come to Grow Weeds

The essence of our self was born into what I call the container of our body. We tend to think of our container as our true self because wherever we go, it is with us. Your container includes all your non-physical aspects: thoughts, likes, dislikes, emotions, talents, hopes, dreams, wishes, expectations, and more—effectively everything that makes you *you*. Within the container, too, are your various potentials—the *you* you could be without sabre-tooth getting in the way. Think of these non-physical aspects and potentials as the seeds of nourishment within you. Each of these seeds has the potential to grow into a beautiful flower or a deeply nourishing plant. You are your best self when you honour the truth within our own container and bring to life all the seeds of beauty within you. You're able to bring to the world everything you have to offer when the thoughts, feelings, beliefs, and opinions that occupy your container are your own. Only then can you even *know* the truth of all of those aspects of yourself.

We are born within the context of a family, each member of whom has her own container. Very early in life, the caregivers in our lives begin to fill up *our* container with the nonphysical aspects of themselves. They place their weeds—thoughts, feelings, expectations, fears, and worries—into *our* container. Some of those beliefs and feelings are about us, others concern the world at large. They aren't weeds because they are necessarily bad, but simply because they are not truly our own seeds. Our caregivers do not do this because they want to harm us, but rather because they feel closer to us when they perceive us to be like them. Parents want their kids to be like them. That's normal and natural.

Because we are so young and so deeply wired for love and connection, we allow them to put their weeds in our container. Sometimes, in fact, we aren't even aware that their stuff *is* a weed. We might realize something doesn't feel right, but we struggle to understand what is happening. Our parents essentially say, "Here, be like this, and I'll love you." So, because we want to be loved, we say, "Okay," and accommodate them. We alter our true selves to make room for the stuff dumped in our container, and we suppress our own. Our need for love and acceptance is so great that we are willing to do anything to feel it. And the dumping, as I call it, takes on an added dimension as we get older.

As we grow up, we become aware that others also have thoughts, emotions, likes, dislikes, preferences, hopes, dreams, and expectations—their own containers with their own plants, and weeds inside them. So, it begins to seem obvious that if we steal the thoughts and feelings of others and figure out what they want from us, we can achieve that love and acceptance we so desperately seek. In service of that need for love, we develop a hyperawareness of others' thoughts and feelings. And our need for the experience of love and acceptance leads us to try to control others' thoughts and feelings. To do this, we must figure out what that person likes and wants and adjust ourselves to meet that other's needs. In a way, it's as if we out of our own container, jump into theirs, steal their thoughts and feelings, and bring them back into our own. Then, we adjust or change ourselves based on what we have stolen. Anything we steal becomes a weed when we bring it into our own container—and we just don't know any better.

The dumping and stealing of weeds into our body container begins early in life and it initiates a pattern of mix-ups—in ourselves and others. The moment we set the pattern in motion, we interfere with the giving and receiving of nurturing. Because we are busy figuring out who we are supposed to be, we cannot *feel* the experience of being nurtured. Nor can we nurture ourselves or others. When we disconnect from what is happening within us and tune our minds into what we think others want from us, we get focused on the weed dumping and stealing. We allow the sabre-tooth to take up residence inside us, and we do something similar with the plants and weeds we have encountered. The hunter-gatherers fought external sabre-toothed tigers and sorted external plants and weeds. We have created *internal* sabre-toothed tigers, plants, and weeds. Imagine that all the potentials within us are our own life-giving plants—and we were born with them. Some of what we absorb from others are also nourishing plants, but others are clearly weeds. Some are thorny and bitter. Some seem sweet but are likely poisonous. What is not truly ours is simply a weed, although it may be a life-nourishing plant for someone else.

When weeds are allowed to grow, they have the tendency to choke out the plants that naturally *should* be growing in our container. The hunter-gatherers had a vitally important ability to discern weeds from plants, nourishing themselves with the wisdom of their collective experience. And we must learn to do the same. The only way we can truly come to know who we are is by nurturing ourselves in the experience we are having in any given moment and by allowing others to do the same for themselves.

How Weeds in Our Containers
Lead Us Straight Into the Tiger's Mouth

This internal disconnect opens us up and makes us vulnerable to the sabre-toothed tiger's storytelling—stories that build up an identity to which we attach ourselves. So, a life process that began with a strategy for attaining needed love and acceptance ends in being lost in a dark, story-shaped world devised by our sabre-toothed tiger.

By allowing others to dump their weeds into our containers and by stealing from theirs, we prevent ourselves from experiencing the love and acceptance we so badly need. The only way to feel that love and acceptance is by being ourselves—but early patterning prevents this. We are trapped inside ancestral patterns that we continue to carry forward.

Becoming aware of these patterns and learning how to nurture yourself is the key not only to creating a different *you* in your life, but also a different future for your children and a better humanity for all of us. As it turns out, our brilliance at figuring out what others want from us isn't so brilliant after all. Yet the exciting news is that we can use that brilliance in an innovative way, making it work for and not against us.

How Nurture Allows Authenticity

To nurture is to be able to see, accept and love what is, without the need or desire to change it into something else. Authenticity cannot occur without nurturing taking place first. And nurturing can only occur when the nurturer is actually feeling love, gratitude, and appreciation for another. Nurturing must actually be experienced *as a feeling* at the time of interaction. To have the capacity to nurture in any given moment, whether it be for yourself or someone else, requires you to be fully present.

With the aid of technology and material wealth, we have been able to augment and replace many otherwise dreary life tasks. But nurture is in a category of its own. While basic tasks of instrumental care can be undertaken by an AI robot, the experience of nurture can only be felt between one human and another. You can pay someone to take care of someone else by doing the basic tasks required for his care. But you cannot pay someone to nurture someone else because that experience lives so deeply in the heart it cannot be made into a commodity. The truth is, at this point in human evolution we are so far away from the experience of nurture that we can no longer wait for it to come to us. I cannot wait for my partner, parent, friend, or child to nurture me. I must learn to face what is inside me in a way that will allow me to bring nurture to myself. It is only through each one of us taking up this growth opportunity, seriously, that we can transform ourselves through self-nurture, and consequently meet each other with open, accepting hearts.

Real Journeys into Love and Acceptance

To nurture myself, I must see, accept, and love what is inside me. But what does that really mean? And if what I see inside is ugly, how can this make me feel better? Surely, I will only feel worse. Those very questions likely indicate that sabre-tooth is up and active and telling you stories that keep you away from yourself. It has you believing the only way to feel better is to resist and avoid what is. Why not? That's how you've managed so far. It's what my client Dianne believed.

Dianne had grown up the youngest of several siblings. Her father left home when she was around eight years old. Her mother coped with the departure of her father through alcohol, and lots of it. After he left, Dianne rarely saw her father, but in her early twenties she began to develop a relationship with him. When Dianne initiated personal growth work in her late thirties, she was experiencing significant numbness on one side of her body. There seemed to be no medical explanation for it. She was also having trouble conceiving a child. She was obsessed with her family and spent almost every free moment thinking about what various family members were thinking about her. She recalled an earlier life of being told by older siblings what she was thinking and what she should be feeling.

In Dianne's case, the weeds that had been dumped into her container were very easy to identify. Dianne's sabre-toothed tiger had taken on the role that members of her family had played in previous years. Her sabre-toothed tiger was very alert to the perceived emotional danger from her family and kept her fight-flight system well activated. The physical symptoms in her body reflected her immune system attacking her own body.

There was a lot going on for Dianne, and she was struggling. She felt guilty for having any negative feelings towards family members and would often say, "They did the best they could." Dianne's sabre-toothed tiger also had her believing that allowing herself to acknowledge the lived experience of her own present life would only make things worse. Having exhausted the strategies she developed on her own, she was looking for other strategies to help her avoid the pain inside.

Dianne's *aha!* came when she trusted me for a moment and really heard my message that her pain was simply her own experience. She allowed herself to see that her pain spoke nothing about her parents' success or failure in their relationships with her. This permission to have her own experience was very significant for Dianne. Here was a brand-new opportunity to feel the pain without needing to explain it away, judge it as good or bad, or wish it had never happened. The less she resisted the truth of the "what is" experience, the more she could feel.

And it hurt—but she didn't die. She learned to be with herself, without the stories in her mind that she had become accustomed to. She learned to allow herself the right to feel her lived experience and emerged calmer, more peaceful, and with less physical numbness. This is nurturing. Dianne has begun accepting herself within her own experience. Those dark parts of her have come into the light—accepted and acceptable—because they are part of the human experience.

Allowing the Good, the Bad, and the Ugly

We are not supposed to only feel the good stuff. We are supposed to feel all of it, across the whole spectrum. To feel it, however, does not give us permission to act it out. To acknowledge it does not give us permission to behave in hurtful and harmful ways. Just because I feel rage, does not mean I have the right to act that rage out. That has already caused too many problems. The experience of my inner world and how I meet it is not the same as the behaviour I choose to engage in. Emotions and behaviours are related, but one does not give permission for the other. What is important in this journey is the process of coming to terms with the pain inside.

All the dark stuff inside is part of us, as is the good stuff. We are meant to come into deep contact with all of it and meet every inner experience with nurture. See it, accept it as what is, in this moment. Meet it with the same openness and acceptance you long to be met with. When we are able to be with all the parts of ourselves—even those we don't want to see—we get to know who we really are.

Right now, you may believe that who you really are is unworthy, having nothing to offer. Remember, however, that that is the story of the sabre-toothed tiger within you. Thinking he is your friend, he believes you need to be protected. You don't. If you did, you would not be reading this.

The Drive to Thrive: How We Got Diverted

We house an inherent pattern of moving forward a step or two and then running back to a familiar place. Those two natural tendencies are actually wired together. We are wired to explore, expand, grow, but also remain connected to our primary caregiver. When we were really little, we did explore, exactly as we are programmed to do, and as we began that exploration we were told, "No!" We were given clear directives to *stop* exploring. This was not because our parents were trying to hurt us; they did the best they could. Rather, it was because our parents were concerned about two things. Worried for our safety, they did not trust our child's intuition to stop ourselves short of danger. Second, they were concerned with how a misbehaving child would make them appear to others. As a result, exploring and growing came to feel dangerous. When you are little and your parent tells you to stop, you'd better do what you are told. After all, you want them to love and accept you, don't you?

For many of us, this early conditioning and patterning reveals itself as we begin to grow psychologically. Sometimes, the patterning repeats itself as soon as we begin to think about growing. The *No* we heard so much when we were little has, in adulthood, taken on a more sophisticated voice and a compelling story. Typically, it's about unworthiness: "You're not worth it; you don't deserve to have good things happen to you." The inner response to messages of unworthiness is shame.

Many of us send ourselves shame messages most of the time. The early patterning of unworthiness and shame that made its entrance when we were misdirected from our natural tendency to grow and thrive, carried itself forward in our inner world. As a little person, far too often we interpreted the *No* as meaning, "No, you are not worthy of thriving or exploration," or "No, I don't trust you," or "No, you don't have the ability."

You can see how that drive to gets extinguished. In the process, sabre-tooth tells his stories of shame and unworthiness and the fight-flight centre is once again activated. Exploration, growth, and thriving are shut down before they even really begin.

Still, despite all this going on at any given moment, there remains a flicker inside us that causes us to take a course, read a book, expand ourselves somehow. It is miraculous really and it speaks to our tremendous resilience as humans. No matter what, we are hardwired for growth.

We come to know ourselves through exploration of the outer and inner worlds. If exploration is associated with being told, "No," and that is a threat to feeling loved and accepted, it does not bode well for us to get to know ourselves. The *no* experience leads us to think we are worthy only of taking direction from others. This is where many of us are trapped and why most of us feel the way we do.

Most of us are fearful of stepping out, being seen, and allowing ourselves to shine. We don't feel nurtured enough to truly feel we have something to offer. This harmful patterning gets passed through generations, not because we don't want better, but because we don't know how to do better.

Wanda is a beautiful young lady who lives behind significant anger and fear. She grew up in an emotionally abusive home and received the *No* experience frequently. Her parents were well-intentioned, doing their best to manage the significant life struggles they endured with the limited emotional resources they had. Deeply affected by this, Wanda sought personal growth after experiencing some significant life stressors.

At the outset of our work together, her armour was very thick and remained that way for some time. She had decided it was better to be angry than to be in the true pain of feeling that she had not been "enough" for her parents or anyone else she encountered. She knew this way of thinking was hurting her and standing in the way of her moving forward, but she didn't know what else to do.

Wanda was terrified of growth. Growth had always seemed unsafe. Even though growth was exactly what she wanted, she didn't know how to allow herself to grow. Bringing nurture to the "what is" experience helped. Things started to shift, and growth began to feel safer. During meetings, Wanda's pain, shame, and unworthiness would again reveal themselves following each growth experience. Her early patterning had been strong, but she ultimately learned to acknowledge that terror and see the roots of it. Wanda had to overcome the emergence of the *No* experience again and again, but each time it became a little easier.

Wanda's situation is true for most of us. We want to thrive desperately, but our patterning has left us feeling we're not worthy of thriving. When you are able to see that the reason you want to run away and hide is a result of the early *No* experiences in your life, that tendency to run away looks very different. It's not so much that you want to run and hide, rather it's what you learned to do in order to secure love and acceptance. Understood this way, it all makes sense. It's not natural to run from thriving, yet so many of us do. It becomes natural when we hear "No!" too often.

You can see why an impulse you cannot help but experience wrong instead of right, bad instead of good. Yet that bad feeling has nothing to do with your worth. It comes from being told you were doing something bad when you were doing something natural and good. I'm sorry it took until now for you to hear that message. I'm sorry you have been shackled within that framework. I am sorry it has so significantly impacted your life. The good news is that you can learn how to nurture yourself through it and thriving can begin to feel good in every way.

Part Two: Now What?

Presence

3

So far, we've looked at what has been happening in the mind and the body to bring you where you are today. At some point, you lost contact with your true self—for good reason. You were, after all, searching for love and acceptance. Nevertheless, nothing can change until you re-establish contact with yourself. You will simply and mindlessly repeat old patterns if you do not.

It's not enough to know about your sabre-toothed tiger and the weeds in your body-container or that you were told "No," too often as a child. Understanding all that may satisfy your intellectual curiosity, but it moves you no farther ahead in the process of freeing yourself from the patterns. Knowing that you inherently do something you no longer want to do is not enough to create change. If it were, we would have very few harmful habits.

Habits are patterns developed in the unconscious, and—as its name suggests—the unconscious is outside of our awareness. Interestingly, the unconscious has a good deal of control over us, but we seem to have little access to it. Knowing you do something habitually is not the same as being aware that you are doing it *as you are doing it*. That awareness can only be developed through awakening an important part of the brain—the prefrontal cortex.

The prefrontal cortex is the most sophisticated of all the brain's regions and was the latest to develop in the evolutionary process. While the whole brain is plastic and can and does change following birth, the prefrontal cortex continues to develop in its essential functions as we continue to grow. When well developed, the area is extremely powerful, offering us a way out of the negative processes I've described in previous sections of this book.

Just as the problem lies within us, so does the solution—but not at the same level as the problem. Too much thinking about the wrong stuff got us here. More thinking is not the answer. In fact, it's the opposite. The secret? Stop the thinking entirely and nurture something that will awaken the prefrontal cortex: presence.

Presence: The Here and Now of Your Inner World

Right now, there is a world of experience inside you, including emotions and physical sensations. You most often feel them in the form of a physical constriction or tightness in the body, and your body "experiences" them continuously. In Part 1, I described how you had to disconnect from your body's experience in order to survive. Because it was too difficult to see how to give others what they wanted from you and at the same time stay in touch with your own inner experience, you chose to disconnect from yourself in order to get what you thought you needed.

The process of getting back in touch with what is happening in your inner world is one I call "presence." Presence is here-and-now awareness of your inner experience—physical sensations, emotions, and thoughts—and it is a fundamental part of the nurturing process. You cannot nurture if you are not present. Nurture, in fact, is a natural outcome of presence, requiring no additional effort or action. Learning how to be with what is going on inside—how to be present—allows you foremost to nurture yourself. You can then meet others and the world from this place of inner connection.

The Practice of Presence

Cultivating presence, as you might imagine, is a lot easier said than done. It takes practice. I always start by slowing down. Like most people, I tend to think too fast, act too fast, eat too fast, do everything I do too fast. We tend to be in relationship with life in an urgent kind of way. And if we are not, others often scold us for being too slow.

In the practice of presence, however, slow is good. When we are too fast, we cannot be present. Racing around in your thoughts is a sign that sabre-tooth is storytelling and you are listening. When you feel distracted by your thoughts or lost inside them, you have given over your capacity to be present to sabre-tooth. He has the stage, and you are fixated on the story in that moment. This is how most of us live our lives. When we are lost in thoughts, those thoughts tend to make us feel emotional danger, which results in activation of that fight-flight centre. But when we are present with the experience within, we are released from sabre-tooth's hold and we calm our whole selves.

A Method Out of Madness

Attending to yourself does not mean listening to the busy-ness within your mind. Slow down and feel something instead. I like to start with my feet. Meet your feet. (If your feet seem too far away or difficult, you can begin with your hands.) How? First, bring your awareness inside yourself. Now, take that awareness and travel down to your feet or hands. Don't study them or critique them. Simply *be* with them.

The reason I recommend being with your feet is both symbolic and practical. Your feet are the farthest away from your head. And bringing awareness to the feet is a gesture of reverence for the part of ourselves that both holds us up and keeps us grounded. It is where authenticity begins and presence must begin there too.

This simple practice of stopping and making contact with your feet—via your inner world, does wonders for your practice of presence. Your life won't change as simply as that, but you will have begun to undo the thing that has kept you identified with sabre-tooth and his stories. I suggest you check in with your feet as many times a day as possible. It's a practice that accomplishes several things.

First, checking in with yourself is both symbolic and experiential in the process of coming back to yourself. We are all stuck inside patterning that takes us away from our self and cuts us off from our inner experience of physical sensations and emotions. Checking in with yourself reminds you there *is* a you. This gives you permission to get back in touch—or in touch for the first time—with the experiences inside.

Second, through coming back to your own experience in your feet, you will start to realize how disconnected from yourself you have been. You will begin to feel a self- connection you may have never felt before.

Third, you will become more aware of your sabre-toothed tiger and how much he likes to be in charge. Each time you check in with your feelings, you are doing something other than what you *were* doing. You are interrupting that which is getting in the way of being in natural connection with yourself. In order to change something you have to interrupt the pattern you are in. If you automatically brush your teeth a certain way every day and then one day you change, you will become aware of your tooth-brushing experience in an entirely new way. The exercise of checking in with your feet serves to interrupt all that sabre-tooth is up to when you are *not* checking in with your feet.

Simply put, the process of checking in with yourself many times a day, every day, will begin to awaken the most powerful part of you and change your brain's neural patterns that are keeping you stuck. Not bad for a tiny exercise that solely makes use of what is already there. As you bring your awareness to your feet, you engage in something other than listening to the stories within. Through this remembering, the prefrontal cortex begins to develop—and presence develops along with it, something that forms the root of significant growth.

Power

4

T he most powerful part of you is your presence, meaning that you are fully here, attending to the experience that's happening in your whole self. When you are present, you *are* your emotional state, aware of how your physical body is holding that emotional state, and you accept all of it as it is.

An eloquent woman attended her personal growth process. She was in her late forties, a married professional, with four children. Liz could see that her marriage was collapsing and wasn't sure whether that was a good or bad thing. She felt pressure from her husband to be more involved in the marriage—more loving, more committed, more engaged. Liz felt bored. She enjoyed her relationships with her female friends and her time away from her husband more than her time with him. There were lots of weeds growing in her container. She felt responsible for her husband's happiness and feelings, and he fully endorsed this with his words and actions. Her sabre-toothed tiger was in full force, telling her stories of what would happen if the marriage ended and other stories of what would happen if it did not.

Liz was lost, confused, and fearful. At my suggestion, she began paying attention to her feet. She immediately noticed a shift in her experience with her children. Within one week of bringing her awareness to her feet, she was able to report how much more connected she felt with her children. With each child, she felt as if she was really there in a way she had never felt before. And her children noticed, too. They responded to her presence in a powerful and loving way. Those relationships were immediately richer. This is the power of presence.

Within that first week, Liz also became aware of how difficult it was for her to find connection with her feet when she was with her husband. She started to become aware of all the patterns in which she had spent a lifetime engaging. She saw herself steal his feelings. She saw him dumping into her body-container. She heard the incessant voice of the sabre-toothed tiger. This is the power of presence. And it is critically important in helping you attend to what comes next—your power.

You gain power when you give yourself permission to feel what you feel. Liz let go of telling herself what she should feel and gave herself permission to feel what she truly felt. At first, she only knew she was miserable. Beyond that she found it difficult to identify any feelings. She spent weeks acknowledging to herself her own experience of life. While she did not allow herself to act out her feelings, she did allow herself to know she had them.

That was step two in this powerful transformative process: permission to be. Emotions are trapped in the body waiting to be acknowledged and accepted. By allowing yourself to feel and experience those feelings in your body, you can process the feelings and transcend them—the opposite of your old pattern. In that pattern, you tried to be who you thought you should be, feel what you thought you should feel, and behave as you thought you should behave.

Your personal power awakens when you permit yourself to experience the truth of this moment. You control neither your emotions nor your physical experience of them. They simply are. But what you do with them is your decision. Until now, that decision has been an unconscious one, patterned through the mechanisms I've described.

Whatever it is, allow yourself to experience it. No thinking about it. No analyzing. No judging. No shoving feelings away. No telling yourself you're good or bad. No waiting for the feeling to be over. No wishing for anything else. Just experience your inner world wholly. Know that in order to be able to lean into joy when it is here, you must be able to lean into pain when it is here. If emotional pain is present, acknowledge it, allow it, accept it as it is in this moment.

I'm not a rule person—except in this one case: *If you want to share the experience with your best friend, husband, wife, or lover, wait until you have processed it.* As soon as you begin to talk about something, you are no longer experiencing it. Your sabre-toothed tiger thinks you're allowing the experience to be, when in fact you're just talking about it. Again, *do not talk about your experience until you have fully experienced it.* Do not trick yourself into thinking you are in your power when you are not. Having come this far, why steal that opportunity from yourself?

I'm not asking you not to share with friends and other supporters. Sometimes you need to talk about an injustice or challenge. But be aware that you're *talking* about something, not processing through it. We've been raised in a consumerist environment that pressures us to believe that answers lie outside of ourselves. We believe a book or friend or therapist or healer will heal us. All those resources may point us in the right direction, but the only one who can take you into, and ultimately past, the pain is you. You cannot purchase presence, but you can practice it.

The Rewards of Claiming Power Through Presence

You will know you have processed the experience when you've felt deeply, quietly, and without analysis. You may have wanted to run away from the feeling but instead managed to bring your presence or awareness to the feeling and where and how you were holding it in your body. In the process, you'll have noted an intensification of the feeling, both emotionally and physically, followed by a deep inner peace and stillness. In that moment, I suggest the last thing you will want to do is talk about it. You'll understand how sharing before processing dilutes both the experience itself and the power you now feel as a result of being truly present in yourself.

What happens next really demonstrates the power of presence. Your heart will suddenly open up. You'll feel a kind of love, compassion, peace, joy, and gratitude you've not felt before. Presence makes things happen that cannot happen any other way. It transforms you into who you are—someone who is inherently open, loving, and honest. A blossoming of self occurs, and you are more whole than before. This wholeness grows each time you confront pain in this way.

This is you. You haven't willed or talked yourself into feeling good about others. You haven't badgered or beaten yourself up. You have met yourself with presence. You have acknowledged and accepted the truth of this moment without needing it to have meaning for any other moment. You have come deeply into living with yourself and in the process your heart has opened up in love, compassion, and joy.

Liz did all this work over the course of several months. She opened herself up to her husband in a way she thought she never would. Now, she's giving her husband the opportunity to catch up to see if they can truly meet each other—for maybe the first time in their lives.

As a human experience, allowing oneself to stay with and transform through pain is vastly underestimated. Allowing oneself to grow in this way is to experience what it means to *thrive*. It is taking a step beyond the lived patterns of merely surviving. Liz held no ulterior motive, and she became so deeply honest with herself that self-love blossomed. As a result, she did not need to be something others wanted her to be in order to receive their love. The love she experienced from others felt more honest and nurturing because it was a love directed to her true self, not her manufactured self. From this new place, Liz found true connection with others.

Truth

5

Practising presence allows you to experience and come to terms with the full spectrum of human emotion. This activates your power, which comes from complete acceptance of what is. Undoing the problematic patterning that has taken us away from ourselves is powerful work. Nurturing yourself through the many emotions and their accompanying physical constrictions of your inner world takes commitment to yourself.

By practising presence you'll be doing the opposite of what you have done in the past. Rather than abandon yourself, you'll stick with yourself through negative and positive, through pain and joy. By committing yourself *to* yourself, you will learn you are loved, accepted, and worthy. And you will have come to this recognition not by reason or self-persuasion, but by direct experience.

When you stick with yourself, you love and accept yourself. You, in essence, make the statement to yourself that you are worth the effort. Rather than persuading yourself that this is the right thing to do, then promptly falling into old patterns built on avoidance of painful feelings, allow yourself to be with whatever your inner world offers. The pain of unlovability hurts, but it won't kill you. The pain of unacceptability hurts, but it won't kill you. The pain of unworthiness hurts, but it won't kill you. Avoiding these and other feelings, however, *does* have the potential to kill you—and sometimes that happens.

Numbing Behaviors

Of the many ways we've developed to avoid inner experience, the sabre-toothed tiger's incessant mental chatter has the strongest hold on us. Why? We are deeply identified with it. We think we *are* the sabre-toothed tiger. We believe everything it tells us. Most of us could not define a self, other than good old sabre-tooth.

In addition to thought processes, the sabre-toothed tiger controls our patterns of behaviour—such as the common behaviour pattern of numbing ourselves to our inner experience. Addictions to drugs and alcohol are obvious numbing behaviours, but other, more subtle numbing behaviours can be just as problematic. Eating, shopping, reading, getting lost in social media, consumption of consumer goods, even working can be addictive. These behaviours in themselves are not necessarily problematic—we have to engage in most of them at some point, of course. But when that behaviour's purpose is to numb you to your inner world experience, it becomes destructive.

What we do is not the problem. The place we do it from *is* the problem. If we behave in a certain way to numb ourselves, we feed the avoidance pattern. If we undertake something as a necessary part of life—rather than to avoid our immediate inner world—it will not present a problem.

The Pattern of Over-Control

A second common pattern of behaviour is over-control. In this instance, sabre-tooth leads us to believe the best way to control our inner emotional experience is by controlling our external world—including, unfortunately, our attempts to control other people. By changing ourselves to give others what we think they need, we try to control their thoughts and feelings so they will like or love us. We try to control plenty of other things as well: diet, exercise, our children, achieving goals, even how we will feel about accomplishing them. We try to control most everything in us and around us. We do this because our sabre-toothed tiger tells us to. He knows that if he can make you believe happiness lies in your capacity to control various aspects of your life, you will be distracted from the pain inside. It works too—until you buckle over in exhaustion.

The Pattern of Creating Drama

A third common pattern of behaviour is creating drama. Sabre-tooth has figured out that if you get busy making a big deal about everything, you are distracted from the pain inside. We all know people like this; perhaps you even recognize yourself. This pattern shows up in your need to tell a story over and over again, filling in more details each time. When engaged in this pattern, you find yourself speaking very rapidly, building and releasing energy through the telling of the story. You may also notice that you're very committed to the story, as if your whole identity is tied up in it in that moment.

Out of Hiding and Into Your Truth

As you engage in presence with yourself, these behavioural patterns will become clear to you. Even as you read about them here, you probably have an idea as to which you engage in most often. But recall the power of presence. Presence will help you see what you are doing *in the moment you're doing it*.

As I've suggested, begin with bringing presence to your feet, which will awaken that powerful part of your brain that is able to bring you back to yourself. Once awake and working, your prefrontal cortex will help you—the *real* you—to become aware of moments when you are listening to the sabre-tooth tiger's stories and behavioural directions. This is a very big step because it means you are learning to no longer identify yourself with the sabre-toothed tiger.

You'll begin to see that those thoughts inside your head are not you. You'll begin to see that those destructive behavioural patterns you've engaged in are not you. This is a moment of simultaneous liberation and terror. It is a joy to experience oneself as something other than the prisoner of incessant thinking and unconscious behaviours. But if you're not that person you thought you were, then who are you? At this point, the terror may set in. If it does, simply stay with it. Feel it in your body. Acknowledge the emotion as the truth of this realization. Accept the realization as the truth of this moment. The emotion will pass and something else will emerge: love. And within that love, you will experience many other heart-opening emotions.

Standing Tall Outside the Wall

You are now stepping into who you really are—a whole person who is able to use your mind as a tool, who feels his or her connection with all of humanity, someone able to feel love and compassion, gratitude, joy, and peace. You have grown into a person who can use your mind and the thoughts within it to bring something to humanity rather than protect yourself from it. This is the authentic you. And by connecting deeply with yourself and sticking with yourself through all the painful stuff, you have emerged as a whole and integrated being ready to live in the world in a new way.

Until now, you've lived your life dependent on defenses and armour. The sabre-toothed tiger has believed you are in danger, always, and in all ways. To keep you protected, he has filled you with defenses that have separated the you with whom you formerly were identified and the *real* you. In a sense, the real you has been kept under lock and key, protected. The defensive you, full of ideas and behaviours generated by the sabre-toothed tiger, has been running your life. Until now, you've been led to believe this is the real you, but somewhere inside, you knew otherwise.

The real you found ways to keep you a little bit aware until the time was right. And now you've picked up this book. Each person is different in her process of life. There is no right or wrong, only what is. Your time is now.

Congratulations! The treasured you is waiting to emerge. Next, we look at what you need in order to prevent sliding back into hiding.

Vulnerability

6

E ach of us inherently wants to know what is going to happen next. In fact, we are somewhat obsessed by it. If I do this, what will happen? If I do that, what will happen? And on and on. We find it impossible to accept the reality that we have no control over what will happen next. So, we try to create a sense of control. And as we've seen, sabre-tooth is an expert in this department.

By contrast, to be vulnerable is to be able to surrender to what will happen next. It is to be so fully honest and accepting of what is in this moment that time and space feel suspended. It is as if there is no *next*. This is all there is. Nothing else. In this moment of deep honesty, self-acknowledgement and acceptance, the rest of the world does not matter. Time does not matter. The circumstances of your life do not matter. The only thing that matters is that you have allowed yourself to be.

Finding Honesty in Feeling

To be vulnerable is to be without defenses. To be without defenses is only a bad thing if you feel you need them. It is legitimate and appropriate to have defenses when you are under attack. But to keep up defenses out of a vague fear of *future* attack simply exhausts you and interferes with your ability to truly defend when necessary.

One of the hardest things in the world is to be honest with oneself. All that chatter in your head is a defense, a way to keep you from being honest about how you are really feeling. To finally allow yourself that honesty and vulnerability, the first thing you need to do is lower your own defenses. This requires honesty with yourself about what you are truly feeling in any given moment. And the only way that will ever feel safe is if you are also willing to let go of judging yourself when you are being honest. Being willing to admit anything to yourself without judgment fosters an environment of safety within you. And where there is safety, vulnerability is not a problem.

We live in a defensive world, where almost everyone is defensive—first, defensive against herself and, as a result, against everyone else. When have you ever heard the message that it is okay to feel angry, despair, hurt, worried, confused, bewildered, or sad? When have you been given permission to simply *feel* what you feel without trying to make sense of it or change it into something else? For most of us, never.

If we have never been given the "it's okay to feel" message, neither have we been taught that vulnerability is okay. Rather, we have been directed to use strategies to avoid the pain. We have been told we really shouldn't feel the way we do or that it doesn't make sense to feel what we feel. We have been shown how to distract ourselves from our feelings. The basic message is that feelings are dangerous and we should defend ourselves against them. Having received this message hundreds of ways, thousands of times, we've become experts in self-defense—against our own emotions.

That is exactly why, when we do the opposite, we transform. When you do more of the same, you get more of the same. But when you do the opposite, you get the opposite. You go from being a defended, disconnected human being to an entirely present and vulnerable person. And you no longer think about life in terms of "should." You no longer need to cultivate the qualities of compassion, gratitude, joy, trust, and authenticity. They are the natural byproducts of being fully present and vulnerable in yourself.

Hang In With Yourself

To be vulnerable is to be without defenses. It means that you embody the process described above. You work at becoming present with the emotional and physical experiences inside you. When those experiences are difficult, you stick with yourself. You acknowledge the whole experience—the emotions themselves and tightness in your body that has contained those emotions for so long. You allow yourself to accept your experience in any given moment as the truth of your experience. You stay present and nurture yourself as if you have just found a long lost piece of you that is becoming reconnected to the rest.

You don't care in that moment what the rest of the world might have to say about your honouring and self-nurturing. The rest of the world is not you and cannot know your lived experience. You are the only one qualified to be an expert on that. What the rest of the world thinks doesn't matter. You are exploring uncharted terrain, and this time no one, not even you, will stop your exploration. You are moving out of surviving and into thriving. You are meeting yourself and you are perfect, as you are, in this moment. Don't change a thing. Stay present.

Whatever is going to happen next will happen. That is vulnerability. And vulnerability is pure, unadulterated truth. No one can give that to you until you have given it to yourself. Once you have given it to yourself, no outside source is needed.

Part Three: The Revolution

Meeting the Wisdom Within

When I began to travel inward in an effort to contact my inner emotions and physical sensations, the biggest hurdle was my interfering thoughts—thoughts about dinner, laundry, things I *had* to do, my kids, my husband, even something a coffee barista had said to me earlier that day. But none of these thoughts, not one, was relevant to *life*. I could pretend that every thought was important and in need of my focused attention, but the truth was quite the opposite. The closer I came to learning how to attend to *me*, the more threatened my thoughts became and the faster they popped into my head. This inner battle felt crazy. I was getting nowhere.

At this point, it would have been easy to give up. It can be very hard to feel when your thoughts are so persistent. If you hear yourself saying, "This isn't for me," or "I just can't do this," then your sabre-tooth has done his job, "protecting" you from the experience of the inner world. And you have succumbed to his command. How do I know? Because I've been there.

For some reason, perhaps because it was simply time for a change, I chose to persist. To be honest, I was curious. What might happen if I tried something else? So, instead of fighting the thoughts or trying to get the voice in my head to shut up, I changed my approach. I had already been doing those foot check-ins for a full year, and that process had made me curious. Checking in with my feet had helped me see that there was a lot more going on inside me than the incessant thoughts that threatened to overwhelm me. From that place of curiosity, I decided to stop fighting the thoughts and allow them to be. I became more interested in what was happening in my physical body than in sabre-tooth's story-land. I studied my physical experience and discovered that my body was communicating with me all day long.

Wow! What a brand-new world it was. Each time I checked in with my feet, I expanded the survey to a scan of my whole body. I realized I was experiencing major constrictions almost all the time. Within a few days, I grew conscious of constrictions everywhere. Tightness in my throat and neck, shoulders, chest, various areas of my back, solar plexus, stomach, abdomen, hips—I was a mess!

Then, I began to notice that each time I felt a constriction, an emotion arose along with it. My beautiful, wise body was talking to me. It was showing me where and how I had trapped emotional experiences. It was showing me how these trapped emotions were blocking the flow of energy.

It was coming together. Like everyone, all I wanted was love and acceptance. When I thought I was at risk of not feeling loved and accepted, I felt I was in emotional danger. My activated fight-flight centre sent sabre-toothed tiger along to protect me from experiencing pain by telling me distracting stories. With sabre-tooth's "assistance," all my emotions fell into the "dangerous" category, prompting me to steal others' thoughts and feelings and allowing others to dump their thoughts and feelings into my container. All of which kept me very busy thinking. But because thinking alone was not working, I developed other avoidance strategies—numbing, controlling, and creating drama. With my fight-flight centre continually activated and my immune system on unnecessary guard, my other body systems became depleted and compromised.

And all this time, my beautiful wise body had been trying to warn me that I was going terribly wrong. But the sabre-toothed tiger was no match for my body. When I figured out this truly amazing thing, I felt a gratitude for my physical wisdom that I had never felt before. The way out of the crazy in my head was through my body. It had been there all along.

Since the sabre-toothed tiger had been the object of my attention for over forty years, I decided to switch things up. Having worked on awakening presence—remember the prefrontal cortex?—I had developed some skill in focusing awareness on the physical sensations in my body. From now on, I would now give the same honour and respect to my physical body that I had given to the sabre-toothed tiger. As often as I could catch myself, I heard the familiar stories about what others thought of me, about the future, or my kids, and I decided to check in with my body rather than listen to sabre-tooth's stories.

Putting Theory Into Practise

Sounds simple, doesn't it? Well, yes, the concept is simple. But the practice was not. My tiger was not happy. I learned that sabre-tooth is actually fed by our attention to him.

Whenever you give your attention—your presence—to the sabre-toothed tiger, he is happy. Your attention is the cost of his protection. He protects you from the perceived emotional danger of life, and you pay him with your attention. And I now began to realize is that he not only protects you from danger, he also *creates* the emotional danger, or rather your perception of it. Yes, he creates the very "danger" from which he then "protects" you. When I figured this out, I felt utterly duped.

How do you think the sabre-toothed tiger responded to my new insight? Right, he was not happy. But from now on, I decided that as often as possible I would attend to the experience in my body when these stories started to unfold. I would bring the power of presence to the physical constriction and see what happened.

Initially, sabre-tooth left me alone, unaware things were shifting. But before long, he figured out that my new pattern was a significant threat to him. He understood that I was starving him out.

Up to that point I had only known a happy sabre-tooth. I was about to meet him hungry and very displeased. The story telling, as you can imagine, escalated, and the stories themselves became more extreme. Suddenly, "enemies" I never knew I had were attacking from all sides, putting me in emotional danger. Sometimes, the stories I heard tricked me right back into my old patterns. But more and more often, I was able to notice this occurring and take an attitude of amused curiosity. I noticed, too, that the louder and more dramatic sabre-tooth became, the more tightness I experienced throughout my body.

I had decided I would be present with my body, not the thoughts. So, I did just that. First, I acknowledged what I was feeling physically and where. I acknowledged my body's messages about where I had trapped emotions. If there was any clarity around what those emotions were, I acknowledged that, too. Next, I moved from acknowledgment to acceptance. These trapped emotions and the resulting physical constrictions were part of my lived experience. I wanted to accept that fact and I wanted to allow myself to feel them fully. So I did, and it hurt a lot, a lot of the time. But I knew I was doing the right and honest thing.

Every time I repeated this process, something shifted inside. I started to become me. I began to feel that this long-disconnected body belonged to me. But I wasn't going to make the same mistake I had made with my thoughts. I wasn't going to allow myself to experience them with my body as I had with the thoughts. My body connection was not a possessive experience. Instead, it emerged as soft and gentle gratitude to my body for all the work it had done to get me on track. I was able to hold an attitude of open wonderment about the whole thing. Each time I was truly present with a physical constriction, it would eventually shift and a release would happen. My body was doing the work of processing trapped emotional experiences, and I was the witness. I was left with peace and joy.

From "Me-As-Thing" to "Me-As-Process"

The attention I had paid to the sabre-toothed tiger had left me feeling identified with my thoughts. Although the content of those thoughts would change, there were certainly consistent patterns in my thinking. As I continued the process of disengaging my identity from my thoughts, I realized something even more harmful had occurred. I had come to see myself as a static, solid being. I had believed that knowing *who I am* meant knowing and committing to my thoughts and opinions. I would only change my mind about a subject with great reluctance. Somewhere inside, I had made a commitment to the sabre-toothed tiger. He and I were one and the same, which meant that I had to stay the same, unchanging. I was trapped in trying to prove myself, and it seemed that no matter what I did, I could never get there—wherever "there" was. I never felt at peace or centred in myself. I felt armoured and hardened.

Bringing presence to my physical experience of my body and holding it there until my body did something with that power was very new and different. The ongoing process of experiencing the flow within my body helped me see that I am not a solid and static being. I am a process unfolding. Being authentic is bringing presence to that process and honouring what is, in any given moment. The *me* of this moment has nothing to do with any other moment. And authenticity, I realized, is all about bringing my presence to what *is* and simply staying there.

Now everything could shift. Once I was avoiding nothing, all my avoidance behaviours fell away on their own. I no longer suffered an inner battle about who I was. I had thought I was supposed to be a solid, perfect person. I had been trying to be loving and compassionate as if those were permanent qualities, like the colour of my skin or hair—aspiring to them as if they were goals that could be achieved.

I came to see that compassion, joy, gratitude, or peace cannot be attained, but can be experienced. I had been thinking about each one as a solid state. I had believed that once I managed to achieve any one of those states, I would spend the rest of my life figuring out how to stay there. Or perhaps I would become so perfect that I would be able to inhabit that state at all times. I realized that I am a process, not a thing. I am in process; I'm not trying to achieve an outcome.

There is no outcome. There is only process. The fact that I am a process is true regardless of whether I show up for it or not. It's really all there is, so I might as well show up—and showing up is simply bringing presence to process. It is allowing myself to be with what is, as it is, in each and every moment. To acknowledge it, accept it, and hold my presence within it brings me first into honest relationship with myself, which then allows me to be in relationship with others and all of life from a place of inner truth. If something makes me feel uncomfortable, the presence that I hold within myself allows me to be aware of that, then use my mind to decide what to do about that discomfort.

Learning to Let the Body Inform the Mind

A perfect illustration of this occurred with Laurie—a beautiful young lady in her late twenties. She had spent her whole life trying to be happy and cheerful. She listened to positive-thinking lectures every day, telling herself that her life was great. She was referred to her self-discovery process with me by an alternative medical practitioner, who had advised her that her body was shutting down. It was hard for Laurie to even acknowledge her inner experiences. She believed that expressing how she really felt would be a betrayal of her commitment to be happy. She reported that most of the time she felt like a fraud and that it was getting hard for her to be around people and keep up her cheerful façade. Laurie was trapped in her conviction that happiness is an outcome of life. She had identified herself as a happy person as if it were a static state rather than an experience that comes and goes. Despite all this, Laurie knew that something was not right. She knew she could not go on the way she had been.

She quickly took on the presence exercise of becoming aware of her feet. Next, she allowed herself to notice the many constrictions occurring in her body. It began to be clear why her body was shutting down. Her commitment to being cheerful had blocked the flow of energy within her body. She also began to see why she had done that.

She recalled her childhood home in which her father told her that her feelings were a choice and that she was required to be happy and cheerful. The message she received was clear: "In order to be loved, I must be happy." Once her sabre-toothed tiger got hold of that message, you can see how every other natural emotion in her life would become a threat to being loved.

It was hard work for Laurie, but she persisted and began to acknowledge what was happening to her body. She discovered parts of her physical self that were so blocked with painful emotions that she wondered whether anything would ever shift. Slowly, gently, and with respect for what was happening, it did. There was no need to make something happen. Everything unfolded in due course. Each time Laurie brought presence to her body, she was overcome with relief. She realized that her lived experience had nothing to do with anybody else.

This was not about her Dad being wrong. It was not about his betrayal of her in the messaging he had given her as a child.

It was about her, and if betrayal was uncovered, well, so be it. Together, Laurie and I acknowledged and accepted that there is no good or bad. There is no right or wrong. There is simply *what is*. Laurie loved this. She could stop being "happy." Her sabre-toothed tiger was less happy, but it, too, became tamed and over time took its rightful place in helping her to discern real from perceived danger.

The test came in a romantic relationship. Shortly after she began to date someone, she started to feel uncomfortable. Her pattern was to do what she would have done in the past, which was to pretend everything was okay and carry on being "happy." This time, however, her connection to herself had sufficiently awakened the power of presence to prevent herself from doing what she used to do. As she continued to acknowledge and accept the experience she was having in her physical body, she became curious about it.

Instead of allowing her mind to manipulate her, she used it to ask the new boyfriend some questions about his history. She found out information that made it clear that she was in emotional danger from him and potentially even physical danger. By listening to her body and using her mind to evaluate her body's information, she made a decision to end the relationship.

Outing the Lie to Yourself

Have you ever wondered why you keep putting yourself into situations in which you end up hurt? It might be in romantic relationships or friendships or even at work. You put in a lot of effort, but someone else manages to get noticed. You might feel you have no way to figure out if the people around you are harmful or helpful. This is what happens when your fight-flight centre is turned on and sabre-tooth is talking.

When the sabre-toothed tiger is shouting at you that you are in emotional danger, you lose your capacity to discern whether you really *are* in danger. The endless sabre-tooth, fight-flight loop can keep you feeling like you're always in danger. You feel as though you can't trust yourself. The truth is, you can't—at least the self you think you are. That sabre-toothed tiger self is the one you cannot trust. The problem is that you don't know how to extricate yourself from your sabre-toothed tiger. That's what has to change first.

Roxanne was a beautiful young lady who, in many ways, seemed more like a little girl than a woman of twenty-six. She attended her self-discovery process with me because she wanted to sort out some childhood memories of sexual abuse. As we discussed her life, it became clear that the sexual trauma was not the most significant ordeal in Roxanne's life. Her mother, a recovered addict, had left her when she was eight years old to attend rehab for a period of months. Roxanne was an only child, and prior to her mother's absence, she and her mother were inseparable. Her mother was "fun mom." They had done everything together. Roxanne had fond memories of the pre-sobriety mom and missed her. In Roxanne's memory, her mother's admission into rehab was abrupt and very hurtful. One day her mother was there and the next she wasn't.

Roxanne was left with a father who was a good dad, but she didn't have the relationship with him that she had with her mom. Certainly, he was not equipped to know what to do with the pain that his daughter was in.

He must have been going through significant pain of his own as well. Worse yet, when Roxanne's mom returned from rehab, she was not the same person she had been. She was angry because, as it turned out, Roxanne's mother had also suffered significant sexual abuse as a child. Now that she was sober, she was beginning to feel her own trauma. So not only did Roxanne lose the most important person in her life for a period of many months, but when that person returned she was not the same person who had left.

You can imagine that Roxanne's fight-flight centre became activated the day her mother left. Between that experience and the sabre-toothed tiger trying to protect her from the resulting pain, I suspect her fight-flight centre never relaxed. As a young adult, Roxanne took up her own alcohol abuse and engaged in extremely promiscuous behaviour, often putting herself into very dangerous situations.

Roxanne had tremendous unacknowledged pain about her mother leaving her. She was supposed to think that her mother had done a positive thing by seeking help. As a result, she told herself that a very bad thing *for her* was actually a good thing. Receiving help was a good thing for Roxanne's mom but a bad thing for Roxanne. At the time, she wasn't yet able to understand what was going on. No one around her had the capacity to support her so she could process the pain and stay connected to herself.

The day Roxanne was able to acknowledge to herself the trauma of her mother's leaving was the day she stopped believing that something that was, in fact, very bad for her was good. She stopped lying to herself. In that journey, Roxanne worked hard to allow herself to acknowledge and accept all of her experience around this very significant trauma in her life.

As she did, she stopped abusing alcohol. She no longer needed to numb herself. She learned that as an eight year-old girl she had had a right to her own lived experience, and that hers was as significant for her as her mother's was for herself.

Through this work she was able to open her heart to her mother again and the relationship was able to heal. When Roxanne accepted that she had lied to herself all these years, she stopped putting herself in danger. Now, she is able to discern what is good for her and what is not. Interestingly, she no longer looks like a young girl in a woman's body. She's become integrated.

Moving to Discernment

Veronica, an elegant woman in her mid-thirties attended her self-discovery process with me because she knew she had problems with discernment. She had grown up in a home with a very brilliant, loving, and abusive father. He had been married and divorced twice before marrying Veronica's mother. They had three children together and Veronica also had two half-siblings from one of her father's previous marriages.

From the sound of it, her father was charismatic and charming—except when he wasn't. Her parents divorced when Veronica was a teenager and Veronica lived with her mother following their separation. Her mother had a couple of relationships following the marriage and seemed to make poor choices in both. From Veronica's perspective, despite being exceptionally bright and successful in her career, her mother always ended up in relationships with men who exploited her.

Veronica had also experienced exploitation in relationships. She had had a few significant connections and reported that she found herself wondering why she remained in relationships with men who didn't seem to care much about her. She felt very much alone. When we began meeting, she had been in her current relationship for only a few months. She suspected the man was good for her. So far, she said, he was loving, attentive, kind, and interested, as well as an intellectual match for her. So why was she feeling the need to run away? She reported that she felt in danger all the time, even though somewhere inside she knew she was not. She needed to figure out how to relax. She couldn't understand why she had had no inclination to end previous dangerous relationships, yet now that things were good, she couldn't seem to handle it.

My feeling was that Veronica's fight-flight centre had become activated when she was young and living in a very unpredictable home environment. She grew up waiting for chaos to ensue, and it did. Her fight-flight centre was on guard at all times, and the sabre-toothed tiger confirmed the looming danger with assurances that things would get ugly. And they inevitably did. Not only was Veronica ready at all times, but the necessity for readiness was confirmed by events in her environment. You could say that she became an expert at reading her environment. If you think you are always in danger, you are bound to be right at some point, especially in the context of Veronica's reality.

But now, in her present life, that reality was not confirming her endangered feeling, and this was making Veronica's sabre-toothed tiger crazy. Sabre-tooth and her fight-flight centre were both committed to the story of emotional danger. The fact that her boyfriend was being kind, loving, and patient was escalating her sense of danger within. She had lost her capacity to discern. What Veronica had come to think of as her own brilliant capacity to detect what was accurate was simply the sabre-toothed tiger telling her she was in danger. She had never discerned a man in her life as safe. Now, with a safe man in a safe relationship, her lack of discernment was revealing itself.

By working through the experiences in her body, Veronica was able to process her current experiences and her history. As her flight-fight centre calmed down, she was able to use the wisdom of her whole self to discern the truth of the situation instead of re-creating the old story. This allowed her to settle into the new relationship, and it began to thrive.

Discovering What Is Already There

8

Our whole self, our complete potential, is already within us. We've been distracted, that's all. And how could we not be? A sabre-toothed tiger is roaming our minds—and that's distracting, especially with all that's happening outside of us, including life, work, raising kids, and sustaining a decent relationship.

Imagine walking into an antique store jam-packed with interesting things. Inside, one amazing, brilliant, unique, invaluable jewel is tucked away somewhere out of sight—but you don't know it's there. You could spend years in that store distracted by everything else it contained and never stumble upon the jewel.

That's your life. It's distracting you from *you*. And no, I'm not suggesting you should take yourself off on a spa retreat. That would be just another distraction.

Recently, I drove by a billboard that read, "The way we spend our days is the way we spend our lives." I could not have said it better. If I spend my day inside internal or external distractions, I will lead a distracted life with its consequent unsatisfying effects. If I spend my days telling myself I should be someone I don't believe I truly am, I will spend my life inside the experience of failure. If I spend my day numbed by a television or computer screen, I will experience myself as numb. In order to avoid that outcome, we have to make a conscious decision that the time has come to *not* be distracted. But it requires more than willpower to create an alternate experience for yourself. We are not released from habits through determination alone.

Committing and Recommitting to Something Different

The sabre-toothed tiger is not going to facilitate your making a decision that leads to its starvation. If you do choose to commit to something other than what you have known, be prepared for some protest. At some level, it all begins with a decision—a decision to discover what else there is, to live differently, to face fear and discover, or uncover, something else. You will be required to recommit to that decision because, in truth, a decision doesn't actually mean anything until it is challenged. In fact, you'll need to recommit more than once. It's not a failure to recommit, just part of the process. And by now you know you are a process, not a static being.

So, make a decision and then make that decision again, and again and again, at different points in the process. And, when you do, the sabre-toothed tiger will revolt. The insurrection is a counterforce needed in order for you to recommit. When the sabre-toothed tiger revolts, and I promise you he will, one of two things will happen. You will slip back into the land of sabre-tooth storytelling for a while, or you will meet the revolt head on right away.

If it's the latter, you'll be able to notice what is happening in your body. In that moment, you will experience physical tightness. Constrictions. These are trapped emotions from the past. If you can successfully observe this as it occurs, your body will reveal to you what is trapped inside. And the best part of your becoming present is that the sabre-toothed tiger has now actually begun to help you. Not the fake "help" that's been going on for years, but the real thing.

Dealing with Guilt At a Whole New Level

Ryan had done an amazing job of turning his life around after years of marijuana addiction. He had gone through rehab and been clean for two years when he came into his self-discovery process with me. I had known Ryan when he was much younger and deeply committed to his addiction. He could never be present at that time because he was so heavily engaged in distraction. I had worked with his family in supporting them in an intervention that led to Ryan's sobriety.

Now, he was doing well in some ways but was still really stuck in others. The capacity to engage in presence had already been awakened in Ryan, and we jumped in and started sorting out some deeper struggles. He talked about always feeling guilty that he had been given the opportunity to become sober, guilty that he was receiving an education, even guilty about the clothes he was wearing.

Now, guilt is tricky. Although we tend to think of it as a feeling, guilt is actually a story. Guilt is one of sabre-tooth's most powerful tricks to keep you away from the experience of your body. In Ryan's case, this was exactly what was going on. As Ryan talked about his guilt, I could see him moving farther and farther away from being present with his experience of his body. So, periodically, I asked him to pause and check on what was going on physically inside him. When he did so, he felt significant constrictions. By keeping his presence on each of these constrictions, it suddenly became clear to him that he was feeling fear. With the help of both acknowledgement and acceptance, that fear began to process and release. And Ryan felt far more at peace within himself.

By becoming aware that something is happening in our bodies as the sabre-toothed tiger is storytelling, we can discover or uncover what is already there. In Ryan's case, we turned the tiger's story into an ally in the process, not by getting lost in the story but instead by noticing that his body was undergoing a very strong experience as the story was being told. We found fear that we may not have found otherwise. Years, perhaps decades, of fear were trapped within Ryan's body.

Guilt, a byproduct of sabre-tooth's "should" stories, is a common trap. When we feel we should be or do something other than what we are, we feel guilty. Einstein said that the solution to a problem cannot be found at the same level as the problem. Trying to work with guilt on a cognitive level is to keep yourself at the same level as the problem. "Should" and guilt are both sabre-tooth defenses, armour against the pain inside. Focusing on either one of those cognitive experiences keeps you feeding sabre-tooth and his stories.

Understanding guilt and becoming present in your body moves you to a level other than the one at which the problem was created. Einstein would be proud: by facing yourself at another level—i.e. your body—you have found where the solution to the problem lies. In fact, at the level of the body, there is no problem at all, just information about what needs to be processed in order for you to become aligned with yourself.

Disarming

As you begin this process, you will feel frustrated, which is the result of our wanting cooperation, not interference, from sabre-tooth. If you feel frustrated when you hear sabre-tooth's stories, stop listening, acknowledge and accept that frustration experience in your body. In this way you will turn the sabre-toothed tiger into a true ally in your process of self-discovery, self-honouring, and personal truth.

As an adolescent, Kim had lost her mother to cancer. Her parents had separated when Kim was eight years old and she had not had much of a relationship with her father after that. She did see him but did not consider him to be a real support in her life. She had married young and ended that marriage after a few years, having realized the marriage grew out of a need for comfort at a difficult time in her life, not from a space of love or connection. Kim had significant anxiety about everything. She worried about the past, the future, what others thought of her or didn't think of her. She never stopped worrying.

Through her inner process, Kim began to see that every time the sabre-toothed tiger started telling the worry story, it was showing her a whole bundle of emotions trapped inside her body—sadness, fear, anger, resentment, grief, and others. Her sabre-toothed tiger had developed the strategy of feeding her full of worried thoughts to "protect" her from the pain of those emotions. But with the help of her astute attentiveness and presence, Kim began to notice that the stories in her mind became louder when the emotions had surfaced. That would make sense—the need for distraction was greater then. She began to interpret the tiger's stories as a way of signalling an experience that was occurring inside her body, one that required her attention and presence. She decided to meet each experience with such calm and quiet attention that she would feel nurtured in a way she had never experienced.

We likened it to a child who has fallen down and has a big scrape or cut on her knee. A caring, calm, and loving parent would attend to the knee with presence and love. She would acknowledge the wound, clean the wound, and dress the wound. She would give the knee and the child the attention and presence they needed in order for the wound to heal. The more Kim took this attitude toward her own experience, the more gratitude she felt for the sabre-toothed tiger. It was, in fact, her ally as it showed her parts of herself she didn't know were there.

All of the qualities Kim began to embody had been within her all along. She was kind, caring, compassionate, understanding, loving, peaceful, full of grace and gratitude. She was also enraged, resentful, sad, afraid, and vengeful. She was holding all of these energies and many more. As she became comfortable feeling those "negative" emotions, she began to naturally embody the "positive" emotions we strive towards. She never gave herself permission to act out the negative emotions—although she sometimes would, even without permission. As she became more in touch with each of the positive energies, her behaviour followed suit. Over time, she fully processed some of the negative ones.

More and more often, Kim felt herself to be in a space of compassion, love, peace, and joy. She realized that it was not about grabbing and holding onto these energies as if they were tangible entities. Instead, she found herself entering into a kind of flow with them. The various energies—sometimes stronger and other times weaker—would come and go. She now knew her task was to be present with *what is* in the moment that *it is*.

Discovering Compassion Is Real

Remember Simon? The youngest of four kids, he struggled with the feeling of being a chameleon. He spent a lot of time not allowing himself his own feelings toward his mother and father and one sibling in particular. Simon was the guy friends went to for help, and although he would always speak in favour of compassion and forgiveness, privately he didn't actually believe it was possible to feel those emotions. It was very difficult for him to give himself permission to *feel* what he felt. He had been raised believing the only way to be a good person is to talk oneself into being good.

He believed that acknowledging a negative feeling would result in the opposite of what he was striving to be. Then, something so significant happened for Simon that I came close to crying with him. Finally, he allowed himself to acknowledge what was there. Some of it was pretty ugly, but there it was, and he didn't run away or beat himself up. He actually felt better when he faced it. By acknowledging and accepting the darkness, something broke through, and he spontaneously felt a deep love and compassion for his mother, the person he had judged most harshly. There it was, the jewel within him that had been there all along—and this kept happening. Each time Simon faced something big and dark, he began to hold his presence in complete acceptance, and something beautiful always emerged from the pain.

This is the stuff already inside us. Once we are in touch with it, our behaviours are organic. We don't have to think about how to act compassionately or with kindness. We are already in compassion and kindness and the action flows from there. We don't have to plaster ourselves with Post-it notes reminding us to be grateful. We just are. Like the flow of water or the flow of life, these energies are not completely consistent. We cannot force ourselves into grace or gratitude or compassion or love. We can only commit and recommit to meeting with complete presence, acknowledgement, and acceptance whatever stands in the way of these energies and allow the experience to be what it is. We must trust it to transform into something else if and when the time is right.

Out of the Mind and Into the Heart

Compassion, gratitude, joy, peace, and love—these energies in particular emerge from the pain every time. Why? They live in the heart. By acknowledging what is happening in your body and accepting it as the truth of your experience in this moment, you free yourself from your mind. The mind, with the assistance of the sabre-toothed tiger, has been running you and your life to such a significant extent that you haven't known anything else. This shift into process and presence takes your awareness out of your mind and into your heart, where these amazing and beautiful energies live.

The makeup of our thoughts is unique. Every one of us has a unique sabre-toothed tiger. But the heart in you is the same as the heart in me. In a way, it's as if there is only one heart and each of us is connected to it. From the heart, your pain is my pain, your greatness is my greatness. We are all one. And if we are all one, you are not my enemy and I am not yours. I feel for you and do not want to contribute in any way to your struggles—not from a place of pity, but from a place of deep empathy and compassion.

I'm a believer that we can't choose our emotions. Why would anyone choose resentment or anger? I believe we often have the capacity to choose our thoughts and, at times, our behaviour. But when sabre-tooth is running the show, we choose nothing. It does all the choosing for us. Once we tame sabre-tooth, there is some room for choice. How do we tame sabre-tooth? Only through presence and awareness.

When we have awareness of ourselves, we can choose thoughts and actions—but not emotions. They happen on their own. When my adolescent daughter speaks to me with some sass—a very normal and natural teenage way of individuating and boundary testing—I feel rejected, hurt, and disappointed. I can choose to think about it in terms of her developmental stage and be happy that she has some spunk. I can choose whether to ignore it or address it somehow, but I cannot choose what I feel. I can choose what I *do* with how I feel, but the truth is I cannot choose what I feel. It's just there, bang, inside me. There it is.

So, these days I choose to address what is happening in me *first*. I acknowledge the rejection, disappointment, and hurt along with the constrictions in my body. I bring my presence to what is happening inside me and then my heart opens up again and I feel love and compassion for my daughter. I still must be her mother and hold boundaries clear, but the response I get when I address a behaviour *after* I've sorted myself out is a far cry from her response when I try to address it *before*. And amazingly, that holds true even if I use exactly the same words in both cases.

How is that possible? When I sort myself out first, she feels the energy of love and compassion. When I don't, she feels the disappointment, hurt, and anger. This stuff is powerful. It's all about being authentic in the experience. What you do is far less important than the space you are in when you do it. Of everything I have shared in these pages, I feel most passionate about this. *We have to stop faking it!*

The Fundamental Truths of the Heart

Compassion is not an action, but an energy we experience. Only when we are truly in that energy can our compassionate action be authentic. And it's not just you who experiences the difference, so does the recipient. We cannot manufacture an emotion. We can manufacture thoughts and behaviours, but emotions are something altogether different. They speak the language of truth. I have found within myself and others that all these energies—compassion, gratitude, joy, peace, and love—emerge when the negativity within is addressed with acknowledgement and acceptance. It's as if we are nurturing ourselves to the truth of the human experience. The truth is that we have the capacity to experience everything and the responsibility to bring our presence to the whole experience. Only in this way can the best of us emerge. This is the power of presence.

In its ability to melt away the bad and leave us with the good, presence works a mysterious alchemy, in which we transcend the bad and transform it into what ties us together in our humanity. Compassion, gratitude, joy, peace, and love do that. They tie us all together. From the experience of those energies, we no longer feel alone. Through the heart that resides inside each one of us, we feel deeply connected to our common heart.

The revolution comes in awakening our connection with the heart. From this place you will come to know yourself as a being in process, deeply connected to other beings in process. Whatever is revealing itself to you now is what this moment is calling you to attend to. Following this path will take you into an alternate reality. Under the control of the sabre-toothed tiger, you've been stuck inside a "reality" that emphasizes achievement, control, and manipulation. You have had to keep your eye on where you are going and be ready to "attack" anything in the way of your getting there. The previous need for control, manipulation, and achievement will begin to fall away as other, more evolved, parts of you emerge.

Notice What Falls Away
9

We can compare this process to a caterpillar's transformation into a butterfly. As new parts of you emerge, other parts will necessarily fall away. Once the butterfly has wings, it no longer needs the same kind of legs the caterpillar had. If it tried to hold on to them, it might never take flight. We humans are like that. In order for us to fully step into our next stage of evolution, we have to let the parts of ourselves that cannot make the leap fall away. We have to let go of what we have known. We have to let go of allowing sabre-tooth to be in charge, thank him for his role in taking us this far, and understand we're ready to emerge as one humanity working together for our collective greatest good.

We have to allow sabre-tooth to take his rightful role in the balance of our whole selves. We no longer need those little legs that keep us disconnected, making enemies of each other. If each of us steps into this next stage of evolution, allowing ourselves to be led by the energies of the heart, we collectively will achieve much more than we have till now. But this is easier said than done. For myself, I've found that focusing on letting go of something just makes me hold on more tightly.

In the past, when I might have thought about letting go of anger, it effectively made me *angrier*—an experience that came with its own sense of failure. "I don't even know how to let go of something," I would self-critically tell myself. But we can't *will* legs to fall off. We can only bring energy to the growth of wings and trust that the legs will fall off on their own.

Those harmful parts of ourselves will become extinct simply because they are no longer needed. We can only do this by being in our process. I have found that when I get busy analyzing the process and what I have to let go of, I'm back inside the old patterns of over-thinking.

By bringing presence, acknowledgement, and acceptance to what I am experiencing, both physically and emotionally, I have found that some qualities have fallen away on their own. I no longer control and manipulate the way I used to. I don't feel the need to anymore. Each step of engaging deeply in the process of presence, acknowledgement, and acceptance has allowed me to grow wings of trust and truth. The more I am with *what is*, the more I want to be with what is. The fear at the base of these behaviours has fallen away and so have the control and manipulation behaviours in which I engaged to avoid the fear.

Part Four: You're In Something Bigger Than Yourself

Global Change
10

The sabre-toothed tiger that lurks in your mind also lives in every other mind on the planet. The markings of each tiger are unique, based on the circumstances and lived experiences of the person who houses him. Sabre-tooth is about survival, a primitive part of ourselves that relies on competitiveness and accomplishment. But survival in our current context is far removed from that of our early ancestors. They were up against physical challenges that lay in working through the elements of cold and heat and gathering and hunting for food.

The sabre-toothed tiger inside us would have us believe resources are limited, and life is a zero-sum game. "If you have more, I have less. I must constantly keep track of the level of threat you pose and compete with you for every imaginable resource." This scarcity mentality cannot be assuaged by an increase in resources, because the competitive attitude remains, ensuring that others are experienced as a threats. And even if resources *were* infinite, the scarcity experience created by the need-to-survive mentality would still pit me against you. In this framework, even an infinite amount of anything is still not enough.

Sabre-tooth not only thrives in this scarcity mentality—he creates it, but not because he is bad. If he could think beyond survival, he would realize that he is harming his host. What sabre-tooth represents is survival gone out of control. This is something we have allowed to happen. Every one of us is responsible in our own way for handing ourselves over to sabre-tooth and taking direction from him. When we fail to examine what the sabre-toothed tiger has been telling us about ourselves, others, and life in general, then we are not able to change our way of experiencing life. We remain in survival mode instead of evolving into a place of thriving.

Imagine what happens when a number of sabre-tooth tigers come together for a common purpose or interest. Collectively, they're certain they are right. Yet collectively, they are in survival mode. They need competition in order to activate their survival instincts. So they create it—sometimes as competition for a natural resource, a piece of land, an ideology, or a religious belief. It doesn't really matter what the fight is about, it is simply a survival instinct playing itself out. As long as sabre-tooth runs the show, this can never change. Not in a million years.

Put On Your Own Oxygen Mask Before Assisting Others

The job of a survivor is to survive, so sabre-tooth needs to create something—war, famine, poverty, exploitation—to give himself purpose. Think about what your own sabre-tooth has revealed in your journey through this process. What if each of us took up the challenge to tame her own sabre-tooth? What if each of us woke up our presence and allowed ourselves to become something more than what we individually are? The collective "something more" would be mind-blowing!

Your challenge is to first work on yourself. When you do, you step out of the survival mentality in which you've been swallowed up until now. You thrive. And once you are thriving, everything becomes different. No more competition. No more "not enough." No more feeling threatened by someone else's greatness, because you will know their accomplishments are good for us all. You experience yourself as an essential part of the collective whole with something profound and unique to offer. You could never see this reality through the lens of sabre-tooth because he wouldn't let you. Survival thinking kept you small and limited. Thriving allows you to be grand.

Your challenge is to engage in your own process of growth, to awaken presence and bring that presence inside, allowing the qualities of compassion, love, joy, gratitude, and peace already within you to guide your next action. Take your time. There is no rush. It is never about what you do. It is about the space you are in when you do what you do. If you engage in protest, for example, that protest must emerge from a space of compassion and love. To protest from spite or hate would be to feed your own sabre-tooth and the sabre-tooth of others, something that does more harm than good. If you feel moved to start a study group, for example, be certain of the energy that is propelling your action. The right energy is everything and it is what ultimately shifts this world.

From Negative to Positive, Inside and Out

Once you and I take action from a place of love, peace, joy, gratitude, and compassion, everything we do has a positive impact in the world. If you work from that place, parent from it, relate authentically with love, peace, joy, gratitude, and compassion, you cease contributing to the negativity inside you and you help clean up the negative frequencies that surround you in the world. You no longer participate in anchoring negativity into human relationships and the planet itself.

That process describes Sabrina's journey. Sabrina had taken a semester off from university to sort through feelings of anxiety and depression. She had been attending school in another city and returned to her parents' home to get a handle on her struggles. While living with them again, she picked up a part-time job at a cupcake shop. Like many people, Sabrina struggled with fears of being unliked. She began to worry about being forgotten by her friends and peers at university.

Sabrina had already been working hard to attend to her inner experience and one day she came into our meeting with a very clear agenda. She had been thinking about sending a box of cupcakes to her friends at school but wanted to be clear about her true motivation. "How do you know when you are doing something from a positive or negative place?" she wondered.

I asked her to think about engaging in the action of sending the cupcakes and to bring presence or awareness into her body as she did so. She quickly noted a tightness in her throat and chest. I invited her to bring presence more deeply into the constriction and notice what she was feeling both physically and emotionally. Almost immediately, she was able to identify feelings of insecurity and fear. She didn't want her acquaintances to forget her. She was worried they were bonding with each other and that she was not part of things. She wanted to remind them she would be returning and wanted them to think she was a caring person.

I suggested that was a *lot* of fear and insecurity accompanying the simple sending out of cupcakes. She agreed, and we stayed with the experience in her body. When she allowed herself to acknowledge and accept the insecurity and fear trapped inside her, everything loosened up and processed. As she began to feel openness and love, it became clear to Sabrina that there was one friend in particular to whom she truly *wanted* to send a cupcake. So, she did. The action was an organic one full of positive vibration. She reported that her friend loved receiving the surprise. Once again, it doesn't so much matter what you do, as the place from which you do it.

As lovely as the large-group cupcake gesture appeared, it was actually driven by Sabrina's fear and insecurity, and if she had followed through, the action would have generated more of the same. She would have worried incessantly if the gift was too much, or if people thought she was weird. Sending the cupcakes from fear and insecurity would have created *more* for her to feel fearful and insecure about. When she felt an authentic desire to send the one cupcake, Sabrina received that love in return.

An action shouldn't be performed because you are looking for some kind of positive outcome. That would be going backwards into that place of control and manipulation you have worked hard to leave behind. You are a butterfly now, and you don't need all those little legs anymore. An action performed from truth and clarity brings the outcome it brings. It is not for you to control, manipulate, or direct.

Celine had the opportunity to learn this lesson in a lovely way. She was accustomed to lots of anxiety and drama in her life. Newly married, she often worried about her marriage. She knew there were things she and her husband needed to talk about but she was reluctant to do so because of what might happen next. She also commonly tried to imagine every outcome. She played out every possible type of conversation she could have with her husband so that she would be "prepared" when they finally did talk.

While she was aware she was full of worry, fear, and a need to protect herself, at the same time she did not want to have to take any responsibility for this aspect of her relationship. She simply hoped her husband would say, "Of course, honey, I'll take care of it."

I encouraged Celine to imagine starting the conversation and bringing presence to her inner experience of physical sensation and emotion. She did this and became aware of many more feelings, the most significant of which was feeling unworthy. She acknowledged and accepted her entire inner experience and found her heart open up in love toward her husband. Now, she was ready to have a different kind of conversation than the one she had planned.

Celine and her husband had an honest conversation and together they are now working on those aspects of their marriage that need attention. And in the middle of that conversation, he said, "I really feel how much you love me."

This is what I mean when I say this stuff is powerful. You are part of something bigger than yourself and your contribution to the wide world is inevitably tied to your personal "stuckness." If more than seven billion people on the planet each contribute negativity to our shared energy field, that's a lot of negativity. If even one person begins a shift, by interacting with hundreds of others, she might just unlock a door and awaken presence in some of them in turn. And so on. This is how the world begins to transform itself.

The process to which this book speaks is peaceful protest—an inner shift that allows for love, compassion, joy, peace, and gratitude to make its way outward authentically. This shift involves trust that the process will set another shift in motion, one that may be beyond anyone's capacity to perceive or conceive of in that moment. It involves trusting that the outer world will eventually reflect this inner work.

When I Transform Myself, I Transform the World

11

The state of the outer world reflects the state of our inner worlds, individually and collectively. We are fearful, therefore we fight. We desperately want love, therefore we hurt each other in our efforts to make others love us. We battle internally, therefore we battle with each other. We simply need to stop and observe what is happening in the world to understand what is happening inside of us.

A while ago, I came across a short, factual news clip reporting the extreme poverty of a northern town. The video showed how most of the inhabitants survived with very little income and the high costs of bringing in food. I focused on my internal reaction to what I read. The feeling I had was hard to pin down, but as I listened, I noted tightening throughout my body. Grateful for the opportunity to get to know myself in this way, I brought my attention further inward and stayed open to each tightness my body revealed. I began to see that I was feeling the pain of others who were having a painful experience. *Their* despair, sadness, and fear about the fragility of life had somehow found their way into my home. I caught a glimpse of the inner world of others through an openness I had deliberately developed. I began to realize we truly are interconnected beings with one heart that beats inside all of us. I hope I was able that day to ease the pain of others through the love, compassion, and gratitude that emerged from me. Nevertheless, I am grateful for the teaching I was given in the process.

Margaret, a client in her mid-fifties, attended her personal discovery process with me for work-related stress. The work issues, however, ended up being a very small part of the exploration in which we engaged. Margaret was divorced with two grown children, both of whom lived with her. She had raised the children on her own. She was quite close to her sister and parents and had some good friends. She was, however, constantly plagued by worries that the people close to her would think she was not a good person. She visited her parents and engaged with her friends and sister from a place of obligation. Her chronic experience of obligation was the most significant drain in Margaret's life and filled her with negativity. We addressed Margaret's inner-world truth, from moment to moment. She had some very significant insights. For me, the biggest moment was when Margaret returned to our meetings and reported that every relationship in her life had changed, how every person she knew now engaged positively with her, and how they all seemed positive in their own lives. Margaret had transformed herself, and her world had changed.

It would be a leap to suggest that Margaret's personal inner work, along with the work of every client I have ever worked with, has contributed to some significant change in the world environment. Still, amidst all the wars and tragedies, good things continue to happen. I pray that all the Margarets who decide they are going to tame the tiger and shift their frequency to love, compassion, peace, joy, and gratitude are contributing to that positive change.

I am a strong believer in the truth that when I transform myself, the world will reflect that change. That is what prompted the writing of these pages. Every word is written from a place of love, joy, peace, gratitude, and compassion for myself—and for you. I hope you can feel that as you read and as you work. I hope you feel that these are words you can come to again and again when you lose your way and need to feel guidance again. There is something more inside us, waiting to be discovered, waiting to express itself.

Truly, you're on the verge of something big!

Acknowledgements

I am deeply thankful to Andy Warren. Thank you, Andy, for taking on the audio production of this book with so much faith and enthusiasm and for bringing your incredible light to every step of this process. You brought the beauty of the spoken word to life in this book. It was a joy to work with you. Thanks as well to Paul Shatto for sharing his beautiful studio space where the audiobook was recorded.

I extend my gratitude to Russell Martin for believing there is a message in this book worth sharing with others throughout the world. Thank you for your guidance and insight in helping make what I share readily accessible to readers.

I would like to express my love and gratitude to my parents, without whom this book would not have been born.

I have deep love and gratitude for my two most important and constant teachers—my children, Keiran and Mira. You have taught me how to open my heart, discover myself, and always find new ways to grow. Thank you for your love, patience, honesty, and your remarkable spirits.

Finally, I would like to thank all the spiritual teachers who have come to me, in likely and unlikely forms, helping me learn that life itself is our biggest teacher.

Note

All clients' names and identifying information have been changed to protect their privacy.

The information in this book is not intended to diagnose or prescribe medical or psychological conditions nor to claim to prevent, treat, mitigate, or cure such conditions. If you have physical or mental health concerns, please consult your primary health care provider or visit your local emergency department.

In this book, no attempt is made to provide diagnosis, care, treatment, or rehabilitation to individuals, or apply medical, mental health, or human development principles to treat any disease, pain, injury, deformity, or physical condition. The information contained herein is not intended to replace a one-on-one relationship with a doctor or qualified health care professional. All techniques, suggestions, and advice the author provides are intended to assist you by supplementing medical assistance with practical and spiritual advice that supports your well-being.

About the Author

Author and spiritual teacher Roshni Daya was born in Cape Town, South Africa. She grew up in Toronto and was educated at the University of Toronto, Osgoode Hall Law School, McGill University, and the University of Calgary. Although she studied psychology, throughout her life she has been focused on the spiritual realm—in search of inner peace, joy, compassion, and an understanding of how we can journey beyond the busyness of our minds and move into a deeper experience of self.

Roshni's life has been a series of small awakenings as a daughter, wife, mother, friend, and a guide for others. Each awakening has given her a deeper understanding and acceptance of the human condition and a greater capacity for presence, love, and wisdom. Her profound yet simple teachings have helped countless people find inner peace, joy, authenticity, and rich experience in their lives. She believes that the external circumstances of life very positively shift with inner self-discovery and awakening—allowing each of us to evolve with love, acceptance, and grace.

Roshni lives, writes, and works with clients in Vancouver, British Columbia, Canada.

www.ingramcontent.com/pod-product-compliance
Lightning Source LLC
Chambersburg PA
CBHW052206270326
41931CB00011B/2242